Moving to France
a beginner's guide

Eilidh McGinness

ISBN:1542489733
ISBN-13:9781542489737

DISCLAIMER

Disclaimer : Whilst every effort has been to provide accurate information in this guide, and the information included is believed to be correct at time of writing, the reader takes full responsibility for verifying all information. No responsibility for loss occasioned to any person or corporate body acting or refraining from acting as a result of reading any material in this guide can be accepted by the author.

Moving to France, a beginner's guide

CONTENTS

Acknowledgements i

1. Liberty, Equality, Fraternity 1.

2. Property-Rental, Build, Purchase 4.

3. Tax 32

4. Residence and Employment 41

5. Driving in France 53

6. Taking Pets to France 64

7. Courts and Police 70

8. French Customs 74

9. Wildlife 76

10. Hunting 82

11. Wine 83

12. Learning French and Education 87

13. La Marseillaise 100

Moving to France, a beginner's guide

Moving to France, a beginner's guide

ACKNOWLEDGMENTS

Thank you to the very many people, who, in their many different ways, helped me in the preparation of this guide.

Thank you for joining me. This is intended to be a humorous and informative, but by no means comprehensive guide to Moving to and Living in France. I have lived with my children and worked in France for over ten years now. This book is a culmination of what I have learned-mostly the hard way.

Please bear in mind that my experiences relate very much to rural life in the South West of France. A region clinging to its roots, in the face of the increasing commercialisation of the modern world, with a cycle of life, ruled to a great extent by the vines and their seasons.

Here, it is still normal to have a potager in the garden, a two-hour lunch break with copious amounts of wine and maybe even a *sieste* thrown in afterwards. Most shops close for two hours at lunch time on the days on which they are open and almost everything is closed on a Sunday. Many businesses close for several weeks in the Summer for the annual holiday. Working life frequently stops at 6pm for an *apperro* with friends.

If this is a style of life you find appealing as opposed to frightening, read on.

1. LIBERTY, EQUALITY, FRATERNITY

The French national motto is one of the symbols of sovereignty mentioned in article 2 of the French Constitution of 1958: *"La devise de la République est ' Liberté, Égalité, Fraternité. "*

The motto underpins much of French Society.

The motto, liberty, equality, fraternity was born in the French Revolution, although it was not formally adopted by the Republic until much later.

The Declaration of the Rights of Man and of the Citizen of 1789 defined liberty in Article 4 as follows:

"Liberty consists of being able to do anything that does not harm others: thus, the exercise of the natural rights of every man or woman has no bounds other than those that guarantee other members of society the enjoyment of these same rights."

Equality, on the other hand, was defined by the 1789 Declaration in terms of judicial equality and merit-based entry to government.

The law "must be the same for all, whether it protects or punishes. All citizens, being equal in its eyes, shall be equally eligible to all high offices, public positions and employments, according to their ability, and without other distinction than that of their virtues and talents."

Fraternity was dropped from the motto, but reappeared defined as follows-

" Any man aspires to liberty, to equality, but he cannot achieve it without the assistance of other men, without fraternity."

Many other nations have adopted the French slogan of "liberty, equality, and fraternity" as an ideal. These words appear in the preamble to the Constitution of India, enforced in 1950. "Liberty, Equality and Brotherhood" has been the motto of the Social Democratic Party of Denmark. In the United Kingdom, the Liberal Democrats refer to "the fundamental values of liberty, equality and community" in their constitution. Related ideals are contained in the German motto "Einigkeit und Recht und Freiheit" (unity and justice and freedom), taken from the German national anthem.

The idea of the slogan "Liberty, Equality, Fraternity" has also given an influence as natural law in the First Article of the Universal Declaration of Human Rights:

"All human beings are born free and equal in dignity and rights. They are endowed with reason and conscience and should act towards one another in a spirit of brotherhood."

Any attempt to infringe a French person's rights in any way is likely to result in protest in some form or another. The reaction can range from a forceful gesture to a spontaneous mass strike, the only certainty being the infringement will not go unchallenged.

When the pension age was raised in my native Scotland, I, although I would have preferred to be able to retire earlier, could not argue with the math's -people live longer, healthier lives and therefore the practical consequence of that was to raise the age at which pension entitlement would begin.

In France, when attempts to raise the pension age were made, strikes and protests were widespread as indignant workers stormed from their workplace and students barricaded the entrances to their educational establishments, staunchly opposing laws extending the age of retirement.

My eldest daughter is very proud of having participated in the

Great Rebellion of 2010 which took place at the local secondary school or college. Unrest had been building up between three different factions of students, those who were infuriated by the frequent strikes by their teachers, those who welcomed any excuse to avoid class and those who took exception to a rule just imposed by the college preventing students holding hands. A spontaneous trike took place one morning as soon as the students entered the college. Approximately five hundred students took part, sitting down in the reception area and refusing to enter class. Protest banners were hastily prepared and the students sang and chanted, refusing pleas to desist. Finally the strike ended just before mid-day when students and teachers adjourned to the canteen for lunch.

Another example of liberty, equality, fraternity is that it is traditional in France for parental property to be divided equally between siblings in the event of a parent's death. There are strict laws in place to protect the inheritance rights of minors and a French person will express genuine puzzlement should anyone seek to disinherit their children or not treat siblings equally.

Another example relates to property purchase. In France if you buy a property and then sell it again within two years, the person you originally purchased from can make a claim on your profit.

2. PROPERTY-RENTAL, BUILD, PURCHASE

"chacun voit midi a sa porte" *everyone sees noon as his own door.*

PROPERTY RENTAL

Rental property in France is usually unfurnished property. Renting a property first offers an opportunity to ascertain if a permanent move is going to meet expectations.

Fifty percent of the population of France live in cities or the south coast. The rental legislation in cities and in particular Paris and Lille are strictly regulated with additional provisions to protect the tenant. The following provisions relate to the less regulated rural areas.

Most rental contracts are for three years although in most areas short term lets of gite properties off –season are not be difficult to find.

If the lease is arranged through an estate agent-*agence immobilière*, they will normally require the following documentation to prepare a lease agreement.

1. proof of ID,
2. proof of address,
3. proof that you have the means of pay the rent- if you are in employment this will usually take the form of your last three pay slips. If you are self -employed, you may require to produce evidence of your most recent tax return
4. at least one character reference,
5. a guarantor may also be required.

An estate agent usually charges one month's rent for finding the property and preparation of the contract. This is often paid by the owner-*propriétaire*

If the rental contract- *contract de location*, is prepared by the estate agent it is called an *acte sous-seing privé* . If it is prepared by a notaire, which is more expensive it is called an *acte authentique* and has the seal of the state.

The most common rental agreement, which lasts for a minimum period of three years is *un bail de trois ans*. During the three year rental period the owner cannot ask the tenant to leave, unless the tenant breaches the terms of the agreement. The tenant is free to leave, whenever they wish, provided they give the requisite period of notice-usually two or three months. The agreement is renewable at the end of the term of the contract.

If the rental term is for less than three years, the termination date must be specified in the rental agreement and the owner must send a letter intimating confirmation of the termination of the tenancy at least two months prior to the end date. If the owner fails to terminate the tenancy, the lease will be renewed for a further three years.

French tenancy law favours the tenant. The eviction procedure is complex and eviction is prohibited during winter months-1st November to 31st March.

On the date of entry, a deposit is payable-usually one to three months rent. At the end of the tenancy the deposit is returned, without interest, less the cost of any damage for which the tenant is liable.

Before the tenant takes entry, an evaluation of the property is carried out. This is called the *état des lieux*. This involves an examination of every room. Anything which could later be attributed as damage by the tenant should be noted- i.e. if a window is cracked, if there are marks or damage to the paintwork, if a tap leaks. Once the evaluation has been carried out, both the landlord and the tenant sign the evaluation.

Charges

If there are charges relating to the rental property, these will be stipulated in the tenancy agreement and are payable in addition to the agreed rental. If the charges are included in the rent the rental amount will specify that the charges are included. *–charges comprises.*

Charges are the communal charges for the regular upkeep of the building and cover things like stair cleaning, bin charges, common water and electrical supplies.

BUILDING A PROPERTY

PLANNING PERMISSION

There are two stages.

1. Obtaining a *certificate d'urbanisme.* This is agreement that the land can be built on. If the land being purchased does not have a certificate already, a suspensive clause may be inserted in the sale agreement making the grant of the requisite certificate an essential condition of purchase.

2. Application for a *permis de construire*- building permit.

Certificate d'urbanisme.

There are two types of *certificate d'urbanisme*.

1. *Certificate de simple information-* this provides general information on local planning and building regulation but does not provide specific information about a particular plot.
2. *Certificate operational-*a detailed planning certificate specific to a piece of land. The certificate specifies the taxes applicable, any servitudes and pre-emption rights applicable to the land and any construction conditions applicable to the land.

   The application for a certificate must provide a clear explanation of the project envisaged.

   The application is lodged at the appropriate *mairie-*mayor's office. The *mairie* indicate their support or otherwise for the proposed project and the application is then passed to the DDE –*Direction Departmentale de l' Equipment* for final approval.

   If the property is close to a *monument historique* or in a protected zone the application will also be considered by the *Architecte des Batements de France*.

   The application should be considered within two months of date of receipt by the *mairie*.

   Provided the *certificate d'urbanisme* is granted, the application for formal planning permission should be lodged within the period of the validity of the *certificate d'urbanisme-*usually one year, although it can be extended, on application, for another year.

Permis de Construire

The application is lodged at the appropriate *mairie* with the necessary plans. The *mairie* issues a receipt within fifteen days. The receipt provides the reference number for the application, and the date by which a decision will be reached. If no reply is received by the date specified, approval is granted by default.

The DDE consider the application. A notice of the permit

application is posted in the town hall and on the plot of land. If there are any objections, these must be intimated by recorded deliver letter to the *mairie* and to the applicant for the permit. Objection must be intimated with two months of the posting of the notice.

Once permission is granted, two years are allowed for the building work to commence. A twelve month extension may be applied for. The local authority should be advised when work commences.

Déclaration de Travaux

For minimal work on an existing building often planning permission is not required and a *declaration de travaux* will suffice. A form is completed and lodged with the *mairie*.

Permis de construire – required for major building work and any work which modifies the appearance of the external structure of a building and for any change in use of a building, and for swimming pools which exceed 100m2 or have a cover over 1.8m2 in height.

Déclaration de travaux-required for swimming pools which exceed 10m2, all works whose ground work is between 2m2 and 20 m2, (in some urban areas conservatorys and extensions up to 40m2 attached to the main building may be allowed without planning permission) building a fence/wall above two metres in height although more strict regulation may apply near to historic buildings or may be imposed by the local *mairie*.

Interior work-Interior work does not require planning permission but any increase in living space will result in an increase in *taxe foncière*.

Déclaration d'ouverture de chantier-This is a declaration indicating that your land has become a building plot.

The *permis de construire* must be posted on the land. If it isn't, anyone can object to the building work at any time over the next 30 years.

The posting must remain in place and name the architects and the construction firm involved. For the first two months anyone can object to the building work.

It is prudent to take photographic evidence and a witness that the notice has been posted as required.

La déclaration de achèvement des travaux

This is the form indicating the work has been completed. It should be lodged at the *mairie* within thirty days of completion of the work. An inspection then takes place and provided all is well, a *certificate de confomité* will be issued with three months.

For any envisaged project a visit to the local *mairie*, is usually very worth well. The staff are generally very helpful and may assist with the completion of any necessary application forms. They can also advise on the availability of any grants.

PROPERTY PURCHASE

MORTGAGE

French lenders decide the amount they are prepared to lend based on the amount they consider the applicant can repay each month. The monthly repayments for all loans must not exceed thirty percent of the applicant's income if single or thirty three percent of the joint income of a couple.

French lenders will not consider potential rental income from the property in deciding on the amount of the loan. A percentage of existing rental and investment income may be taken into account depending on the lender.

For self -employed applicants, an average is taken of the applicant's income over the previous three years. For employed applicants the lender will base the amount of income on pay slips and the amount credited to the applicants account each month. All outgoings will be taken into account.

For applicants whose main residence is out with France the maximum lending amount is unlikely to exceed eighty- five percent of the sum borrowed. For applicants who are resident and working in France, one hundred percent mortgages may be possible.

A survey is not usually required by the lender although occasionally lenders arrange for a valuation at their own expense in connection with the application process.

Mortgage terms tend to range between five and twenty- five years and can be either fixed rate or variable rate. There is normally an arrangement fee for the mortgage and life and building insurance are obligatory.

Once a lender has decided to offer a mortgage, a mortgage offer is issued. Then there is an obligatory cooling off period of ten days. The offer cannot be accepted during this period. The funds are generally available shortly after the mortgage acceptance has been returned.

SURVEYS

Surveys are not common in France and generally do not form part of the purchase process, although it is possible to obtain a survey if desired. There are surveyors to be found, although they are usually based in larger towns or cities.

DIAGNOSTIS

The seller is obliged to produce a set of diagnostics regarding the condition of the property before any contractual agreement of sale is entered into. The required diagnostics are electrical, asbestos, lead, gas, energy, seismic, termites-in stipulated areas and drainage.

Electrical

A report on the condition of the electricity wiring within the property. A survey is valid for three years. No survey is necessary where a *certificat de conformité* can be produced as evidence that the property complies with the regulations, provided the certificate is less than three years old.

Asbestos

A report on the presence or otherwise of products or materials containing asbestos, - *amiante*. This rule only applies to properties granted planning permission earlier than 1st July 1997. The period of the validity of the report is not regulated although changes in the test requirements may mean that an updated report is required.

Lead

A report on the presence or otherwise of paintwork that contains lead, in a report called the *constat de risque d'exposition au plomb* - CREP. This survey requirement applies to all properties built before 1949. The report must be dated no more than one year prior to the date of sale. If lead is not found to be present, or is found in such a low quantity so as to not be a risk to health, then no further survey is necessary on a subsequent sale of the property.

The survey requirement also applies to the communal areas of a block of flats and to all rental properties let after 1st August 2008. In relation to rental properties the survey must have taken place within the last six years. Where lead is not found, no further survey is required.

If a large-scale presence of lead paintwork is found, the technician is obliged to make a report to the local *préfecture* and the owner can be forced to undertake remedial work.

There is no requirement to report on the presence of lead piping within the property.

Gas

A report on the gas installations within a property -*Installations de gaz*. It applies to those properties where the gas installation has been installed for at least fifteen years. The report is valid for three years.

Energy

A report on the energy performance of the property *Diagnostic de Performance Energétique* – The *DPE* is designed to give the future owner an indication of the level of energy consumption and heating costs. The report grades the level of energy efficiency using the European standard energy efficiency rating scale - A (economical) to G (high consumption) - in terms of the annual level of consumption of energy and greenhouse gas emissions. The report is valid for ten years although changes in regulation may necessitate an updated report.

Seismic

A report on any natural or industrial risks, called *risques naturels ou technologiques*, to which the property may be subjected, together with a declaration by the seller concerning any previous insurance claim(s) on the property relating to a natural disaster.

The report is required in those communes where there is a risk prevention plan (*un plan de prévention des risques naturels*) in place, or in those areas classified as at risk of seismic movement.

The report must stipulate, for instance, if the property is located in a flood zone, an area prone to earthquakes, major storms, subject to ground movement or near a dangerous factory.

The report cannot be dated more than six months prior to the date of sale and must be updated if there has been a change in the designation of the area, prior to completion.

The seller must also state whether they have previously received compensation from their insurer on a claim resulting from a natural or 'technological' disaster on the property, e.g. claim for subsidence, flooding, or storm damage.

Termites

A report on the presence or otherwise of termites (*termites*) and other similar destructive pests in the property. The survey is called the *etat des risques parasitaires.*

This report is only required within designated areas of the country. At present there are fifty five departments where the diagnostic is required. These departments are found in the South-West, Atlantic and Mediterranean coast, departments bordering the Rhone valley, the Garonne valley and the Loire valley and L'ile de France.

If a survey is required, it cannot be dated earlier than six months from the date of sale.

If termites are found the owner is obliged to inform the *mairie*.

The expert preparing the report will check all parts of the house, including the garden, and out buildings, using a punch (to sound out wood) and a sound or movement detector. If termites are found, the seller may undertake to carry out a treatment and this may form a suspensive condition in any sale agreement.

Termites, whose name comes from the Latin 'termes', meaning rodent worm, differ from other xylophagous (wood-eating) insects, because they are organised into a society, rather like ants and bees.

There are over 2,000 species of termite but only seven have been found in France. Five of these are 'underground' termites (Rhinotermitidae) and two are 'dry wood' termites (Kalotermitidae). The worst damage is generally caused by underground termites.

Termites need a water supply in order to exist, but this can be very minimal – even condensation on a water pipe will suffice, or a leak in a poorly maintained wall. Temperature is also important, which might be provided by the climate, or artificially by heating or building insulation. Termites, in France, were once confined to the south but have been spreading northwards as the summers become warmer. Very few departments are now completely without their presence.

Generally, the main termite colony is situated underground – up to six metres below the soil surface. A termite colony takes about five years to mature and may include up to 200,000 workers. These are the termites that eat wood and provide food for the others. The workers dig or build 'galleries', inside, from which they to and fro incessantly, in search of food. These galleries are always free of sawdust, unlike other wood-borers such as the long-horn beetle. Termites penetrate into houses through moisture, but always away from the light. This makes them difficult to detect.

Termites spread either:-

1. by swarming: in the first few days of spring. Discarded termite wings are often the first sign of termite activity in a building, as

they drop their wings once they have found a mate.

2. by propagation: when termites are moved – for instance, in infested wood. At least one hundred termites are needed to found a new colony.

Termites feed on wood and in the wild, serve an important function by converting dead trees into organic matter. However, when they feed on the wood in buildings, they can cause structural damage. Termites tend to attack wood which is moist and close to the ground. They eat from the inside out. They also eat other forms of cellulose, including books.

Under favourable conditions, a colony of 60,000 termite workers can consume a one-foot length of two by four in as little as four months. Under less ideal conditions, it can take as long as eight years for termites to cause noticeable damage.

Termites are like small white grubs in appearance. There are a wide variety of treatments to prevent their infestation and regulated experts available to treat and remove termites in the event of an infestation.

There are some simple precautions to discourage termites in the vicinity of a building.

1. Don't leave waste lumber lying on the ground.
2. Clear downed twigs and branches from the garden.
3. Only use mulch in areas of the garden not immediately adjacent to buildings.
4. Don't store firewood against the walls of buildings.
5. Use treated lumber for any wooden structures which have wood in direct contact with the ground.
6. Use concrete supports between wooden structures and the ground.
7. Ensure any water leak is repaired promptly. Termites rely on a water source.

8. Avoid any heavy plant growth around buildings as this can encourage dampness and therefore termites.

Septic tank

A report on the condition of a septic tank for those properties which do not have mains drainage -*diagnostic d'assainissement non collectif.*

The survey report must have been carried out no later than three years prior to the date of sale. The law requires that if a septic tank is found not to conform, the new owner must bring it up to standard (or at least commence works to bring it up to standard) within one year of the date of purchase of the property.

The most common types of drainage are-

Septic Tank which takes only toilet waste - *Fosse Septique*

Septic Tank which takes both toilet waste and greywater (bath, sink, dishwasher, etc.) - *Fosse Toutes Eaux*

Sewage Treatment Plant- *Micro-Station*

Cesspool which simply stores all the wastewater for regular emptying by tanker- *Fosse d'etanche*

In the past, the French separated the grey water from showers, sinks, washing machine etc. and the sewage from the WC into different systems.

The greywater was often piped into a stream or ditch directly without any treatment.

The toilet waste was either:-

1. piped into a septic tank (*fosse septique*) with an outlet

to a primitive filter bed that normally consisted of a trench filled with stone (*tranchee d'epandage*) These septic tanks are often too small now to cope with the amount of liquid going into them.

2. piped into a *fosse d'etanche* (cesspool).

It has been estimated that the majority of rural French properties do not comply with the current regulations.

In December, 2005, the *mairie* of each *commune* became directly responsible for every aspect of wastewater treatment. The *mairie* also became responsible for implementing the new strict regulations on septic tank systems (*fosse toutes eaux*) and for ensuring the regular maintenance of septic tanks and sewage systems, be it an individual (*non-collectif*) system or municipal (*collectif*)system. The *mairie* has to arrange an inspection of individual systems every four years and issue a report which should be retained.

Areas have been designated either '*collectif* or '*non-collectif*' areas. If an area has been designated a '*collectif*' area, it means that a mains sewage system has been decided upon as the best way of dealing with sewage in that area, even if mains sewerage is not yet in place.

Most *mairies* appoint a professional body to enforce the law. They are often (but not always) known as S.P.A.N.C. (*Service Public d'Assainissement Non Collectif*) and service a group of communes from a local office.

Water bills in France have a charge "*Redevance Service Public d'Assainissement Non Collectif*". This charge is applied by the issuing water company to help finance the implementation of the drainage regulations. The cost varies from region to region.

The main purpose of the drainage regulations are to ensure that all the private systems in existence in France are fit for purpose and do not cause pollution of groundwater or watercourses.

Diagnostics are arranged with the appropriate water authority who send an engineer who will verify:-

1. Location of the septic tank

2. Access to and condition of the septic tank

3. Ventilation of the septic tank

4. Volume of the septic tank

5. Sludge level

6. Drain going to the filtration system

7. Proximity of any water sources, above and underground

8. Filtration system

A report is then issued stating if the sewage system is working correctly and whether it conforms to the current requirements. If the system is not "*au norme*" the report will detail the failings in the system.

If purchasing a property in an area where the drainage is designated to become "*collectif*" the *mairie* may postpone any requirement to enforce upgrading of an existing septic tank if it is anticipated there will be a requirement to join the *collectif* system once it is in place.

If there is a requirement to install a new septic tank consideration should be made for the following:

1. whether there is enough available land, bearing in mind that the drains for a septic tank must be installed a certain minimum

distance from the boundaries of a property (e.g. 3 to 5m), and must cover a certain area depending on the size of the tank (generally at least 85m2).

2. whether there are rivers, canals or other water courses which might affect the siting of the tank and soak-away and the appropriate type of soak-away – for example, a septic tank mustn't be less than 35m from a well.

3. whether the ground is marshy or rocky, in which case installation could be more difficult and therefore more costly.

4. whether the land slopes upwards from the house. This may mean that waste water requires to be pumped up to the soak-away – another additional cost.

5. whether there is access to the site for a lorry (delivering the tank and subsequently emptying it) and a digger to install the soak-away.

Any system is likely to require further treatment before discharge. Many water authorities favour a sand filter system.

There are alternatives to septic tanks, e.g. reed beds, but these must be properly designed and constructed to meet the required standards. The installation of 'alternative' sewerage systems may make a property difficult to sell.

Discharge of septic effluent into a watercourse is illegal.

The most common system for septic tank effluent treatment is a sand filter, which involves a very large hole being dug, perhaps 30 square metres and 1.5 metres deep, lined with heavy duty plastic, then filled with various layers of sand, gravel, and geotextile membranes. The outflow from the septic tank then passes into this filtration system, through pipes spread across the top, filters through the sand bed, and is collected by further pipes at the bottom before being released into the environment.

Application to install a new septic tank.

For a septic tank for a new build property or to replace an existing septic tank, a"*Demande d'installation d'un dispoitif d'assainissement non collectif*" is obtained from the local *mairie*.

The application requires:

> 1.The application form completed and signed with details of the number of main rooms, slope of the land, the ground water level and the type and size of filter bed.
>
> 2. A location plan (1:25,000 or 1:10,000)
> 3. A layout plan showing existing and future buildings, the proposed location of the septic tank installation, any wells or streams and the slope and direction of slope of the land.

> Where the property has five main rooms and under-usually a septic tank of three cubic metres will be required. An additional cubic metre is required for each additional room.

Rules on minimum distances for septic tanks in France

You cannot site a septic tank within three metres of a neighbouring property. It is also forbidden to place a septic tank less than three metres away from trees and shrubs. Despite its name of *fosse toutes eaux*, rain water does not go into the septic tank. Other rules state that you must leave thirty five metres distance between the filter bed of the septic tank and a water source, such as a stream or well. Ventilation is important, and easy access by safely covered manholes is also prudent. It is only necessary to install a fat trap or grease trap if the septic tank is more than ten metres away from the kitchen.

Non-electric sewage systems and upgrades to septic tanks may qualify for a zero percent interest eco loan.

PURCHASE CONTRACT

Once the necessary diagnostic reports have been made available by the seller and an agreement has been reached regarding the conditions of sale, a purchase agreement can be entered into.

The purchase system is straightforward in France. There are several methods of purchase but the most common is to enter into a *compromis* as soon as possible after the conditions of sale have been agreed. The *compromis* is a preliminary contract of sale. It is a binding contract and sets out the conditions of sale.

Any suspensive conditions of sale are detailed in the *compromis*.

For example, if the purchaser requires a mortgage, it is a compulsory condition of sale that the mortgage is obtained. The *compromis* details the dates by which the applicant must lodge the full mortgage application, together with dates on which the seller should be notified of the progress of the loan application. If the mortgage is refused, the purchaser is entitled to withdraw from the purchase without penalty, and any deposit paid will normally be refunded, provided the purchaser has lodged the loan application as required in the *compromis*.

If a purchaser wishes to install a swimming pool in their new property, and this is an essential condition of purchase, likewise a suspensive condition should be inserted in the *compromis* to that effect. A time period will be stipulated within the *compromis* for lodging the necessary application. Again if the application is refused the purchaser is entitled to withdraw from the purchase without penalty.

Similar clauses may be inserted if for example the purchaser wishes to change the route of a right of access over the property or alter window sizes.

It is important to consider these matters at the outset at the time of signature of the preliminary contract as afterwards it will be too late.

In order to prepare the *compromis* the notaire will require copies of at least the following documents relating to the purchaser.

1. passport and birth certificate,
2. marriage certificate if married, divorce certificate if divorced,
3. birth certificates of any children under eighteen,
4. details of purchaser's address and occupation.

It may seem intrusive but the title deed for a French property sets out the purchasers and seller's full names, occupations, dates and place of birth and dates and place of marriage and also any divorces along the way. It is important for their inheritance law system that the inheritance rights of minors are protected which is why the information regarding children is sought.

Once the *compromis* has been signed, the notaire sends a copy to the purchaser by recorded delivery. The purchaser then has ten days cooling off period. During this period the purchaser can withdraw from the sale without penalty if they so wish.

There is usually a deposit paid by the purchaser when the *compromis* is signed. The deposit is a matter of negotiation, but when the purchaser is purchasing with cash and has the funds immediately available, the deposit is usually ten percent.

The *compromis* can easily run to thirty pages and contains many standard conditions regarding property purchase. Both sellers and purchasers are usually present at the signature of the *compromis* and as the process of signature of the document can easily take an hour or more it can be a useful opportunity to get to know the seller and learn more about the property.

If either the seller or purchaser is unable to be present for the signature of the *compromis,* it is possible to authorise a third party to sign on behalf of the absent party. The absent party signs what is called a *procuration* to permit the third party sign a binding agreement on their behalf. The *procuration* details the principal conditions of sale and is usually granted in favour of a clerk of the acting notaire.

The sale process usually takes between six weeks and three months. If any of the suspensive conditions are not met, or if there is a problem with the title, the purchaser can withdraw from the sale agreement and any deposit paid is returned. Therefore, if there is a suspensive condition of sale that a mortgage is granted, and the mortgage application is refused, the purchaser can withdraw from the sale without penalty. However, if the purchaser changes their mind and pulls out of the sale, they risk losing any deposit paid.

PRE-EMPTION RIGHTS.

Once the *compromis* has been signed and the cooling off period has passed, the notaire ascertains if any of the bodies having a right of purchase wish to exercise that right.

Pre-emption rights may be held by –

1. SAFER-*société d'aménagement foncier et d'établissement rural*, have a right of exercise of pre-emption over agricultural land. Once they are notified by the notaire of

the sale contract, they have two months to ascertain whether any of their members wish to purchase the property on the same terms. The two month period can be accelerated on payment of a fee.

2. The *mairie* of the commune in which the property is situated often has a right of pre-emption, although this is rarely exercised unless the sale property is required for public works like a school.

3. In some cases, tenants of a property have a pre-emption right.

4. Co-proprietors have a right to purchase, if one of the other proprietors decides to sell their share.

Once the notaire has carried out the necessary checks to the title deeds – i.e. no outstanding mortgage, no unresolved title disputes, no unexpected rights of way, and all suspensive conditions have been met i.e. mortgage obtained, necessary planning granted, it is time to fix a date for the signature of the final *acte*. This is the day on which the purchase price is paid, the keys are exchanged and the purchaser has right of entry to the property. The date for the signature of the *acte* is fixed by the notaire after consultation with the parties involved. The date by which the *acte* must be signed is stipulated in the *compromis*. The purchase price should be paid to the notaire by bank transfer in advance of the sale.

It is prudent to visit the property purchased immediately before signature of the *acte* to ensure that the property is in the same condition as when the *compromis* was signed. It is advisable to check that everything that is being left is in working order, eg central heating system, pool cleaning system. Any water, gas and electric meters should be read and the appropriate service authority advised of the change of ownership. Schedule for at least an hour for the signature of the *acte*. Unless your notaire has an electronic signature system there are a great many forms to sign.

The *taxe foncière* may be apportioned at the time of sale depending on the practice of the notaire involved.

NOTAIRES FEES

The notaires fees are fixed by the state and generally are between a six and a half and eight percent. Most of this sum is tax. The notaires fees are usually paid by the purchaser. Purchaser and seller often use the same notaire although each are entitled to choose separate notaires if they wish. If there is more than one notaire involved in a purchase the fees are apportioned.

AGENT IMMOBILIER FEES

If an estate agent is involved in the purchase, their fees will be stipulated in the *compromis* and paid to the notaire with the purchase price. Fees are subject to negotiation and estate agents are obliged to declare their level of fees when advertising properties.

INSURANCE

The purchaser is obliged to arrange building insurance for the property from the date of entry.

ENVIROMENTALLY FRIENDLY PROPERTY

By 2020 all properties constructed in France should produce energy. Grants may be available to make an existing property more energy efficient

Contacts

Construction Respecteuse de l 'Environment et Econome en Energie, CREEE

www.cr3e.com

eco-logis.com

PROPERTY STYLES

Some terminology for property styles which may be useful for anyone in search of a character property.

Bergerie- originally a sheep or goat fold building usually located in an isolated location with the ability to hold up to a maximum of fifty animals. Usually the footprint of the building is rectangular. The material of construction usually depends on what was locally available. Usually the windows are very small to retain heat.

Belle Demeure – elegant period property.

*Chais-*Large room used to store, ferment and produce wine. Usually has an earth floor as the humidity assisted the fermentation of the wine.

Chartreuse – originally a long building used as a monastery. Usually there are rows of tiny rooms where the monks slept. Originally they were completely secluded. In south-west France secluded cottages are also called *chartreuse*.

Chaumiere –a thatched cottage. Straw stubble is *chaume*.

Originally these cottages were inexpensive builds constructed with local materials. Earth, wood, stones and thatch from local crops.

Colombage - these are wooden uprights of oak. Buildings were constructed by placing the uprights in the ground and filling the open area in between with local materials, a mixture of straw, clay, mud and water called *torchis*. Small red bricks-*brico* and stone are also used depending on the region of France.

Donjon - a tower that is attached to a building and may date back to the 11th century. Originally this was the most solid part of a castle and would have no entrance on the ground floor. The earliest donjons have a rectangular footprint although later styles have round, and hexagonal shapes.

Fermes –original farms consisted of one room, divided into two sections, in which owner and animals sheltered. As farms developed so did the size of the owner's residence and the extent of the outbuildings for the animals. Many farms have been converted to luxury gites and there are a wide variety of styles of buildings according to the region of France.

Fermes a cour fermee- enclosed courtyard farm-this type of farm usually formed a large estate and required numerous staff. There is usually a large entrance into the courtyard and the main dwelling house is situated opposite the entrance. Originally the buildings on the perpendicular sides of the courtyard were used for housing the animals and the barn was closest to the entrance.

Gentilhommiere – a luxurious summer home for a nobleman. Usually large and spacious.

Girondine-house, typical of the Gironde region of south-west France, built typically with blonde sandstone blocks.

Maison Bourgeoise-spacious village house with a walled or fenced garden.

Mas –one or two story farm with barn or stables

Maison de Maitre- a spacious manor house with enclosed park, found rurally or in small towns. Typically, three floors with the reception rooms on the ground floor, the private rooms on the middle floor and the servant's quarters on the top floor under the roof.

Manoir- Impressive residences constructed by feudal lords who had not been authorised to build castles with watchtowers.

Moulin- mill

Longere- typically a long rural dwelling, found in many regions in France.

Pigionnier- a structure originally used to house pigeons or doves. They can be built onto the end of a house, barn or other outbuilding or a completely separate structure. Usually there are pigeonholes for the birds to nest.

SWIMMING POOLS

Inground swimming pools are legally required to have either a safety fence built around them or a swimming pool alarm. The fencing which meets the required legal requirements is expensive so many people opt for the much cheaper pool alarm.

Inground swimming pools require a *declaration de traveaux* if the surface area is between 10m2 and 100m2. Less than that and no permission is required. If the pool exceeds 100m2 in surface area or if it has a cover with a height in excess of 1.8m2, planning permission is required. For inground pools, the surface area of the pool is added to the recorded habitable surface of the house thereby increasing the *taxe foncière* of the property. As a result, *hors sol* or above ground pools have become more popular. If an above ground pool is partially inset to the ground, or inset on a slope with decking, a look very similar to that of in ground pools can be achieved, at a fraction of the cost.

If it is intended to rent out the property or use part of the property as a *gite,* then, it will probably be desirable to have a pool. (Depending on the region of France)

There are two types of pool. A liner pool has a liner sheet covering a base and is much cheaper to install than a concrete pool which will usually require a professional builder to install.

A swimming pool requires regular maintenance. Salt pools are generally more expensive to maintain than chlorine pools as a result of the corrosive nature of the salt.

Generally, the PH level of the pool should be checked at least once a week. Many inground pools have an automatic cleaning system which makes the maintenance much easier.

It is prudent to keep any swimming pool as far away as possible from any plants which have deciduous leaves which are likely to end up in the pool and add to the cleaning.

Summer covers can be used to slip over the pool, if a cold night is anticipated to maintain the water temperature. Winter covers are used to cover the pool, when it is closed over the winter.

Installing heaters can extend the use of the pool by around a month at each end of the season.

Automatic swimming pool vacuums are a worthwhile investment to minimise cleaning time and maximise leisure time.

Hot Spas and lazy spas are becoming an attractive alternative to a swimming pool for those who have little space or don't want to make the investment a swimming pool requires.

If a swimming pool isn't enough and your French dream includes a lake:-

LAKE

Lakes in France should be registered with the Department of Agriculture and fall into fishing categories (*categorie piscicole*). Many lakes are not registered, particularly if they are not fed by a running stream and rely on rainfall for their water content.

If it is intended to offer fishing from a lake, that lake should be officially registered. If purchasing a lake, ensure that all necessary permissions are in place for the intended use.

It is straightforward to register a lake. The appropriate department is the *Direction Départmentale de l'agriculture et de la Foret,* which is usually located at the prefecture.

For most purchasers the preferred classification is Category 2, which is 'closed.'

This basically means that night fishing is permitted and no fishing licenses are required.

To be classified as closed, the lake cannot have a stream running through it. Therefore there is no risk of free movement of fish, to and from the lake. If there is a stream running to and from the lake, it may be possible to re-direct a stream to achieve a 'closed' status, however this involves submitting a detailed project request.

Lakes with a stream running through them are subject to annual inspection and water testing.

Draining a lake

Permission should be obtained to empty a lake, even partially. This usually takes approximately a month to obtain.

3. TAX

"vaut mieux prevenir que guerir" –it is better to prevent than to heal.

France is known for having high taxation-so be prepared.

French residents are taxed on their worldwide income and non-residents are taxed on their income from French sources alone.

An individual is resident in France for tax purposes if that individual: -

1. spends more than 183 days per year living in France
2. carrys on a professional activity in France- whether employed or self-employed-unless it can be demonstrated that actively is incidental.
3. has a centre of economic interest in France.

Non-resident taxation does not apply to countries which have signed a double taxation agreement with France. These taxation treaties ensure that income which has already been taxed in one country is not taxed again in another country sharing the treaty.

All EU countries are signatures to the treaty as are Australia, Canada, USA and New Zealand

An individual moving to France permanently should notify the tax office in their country of departure. Once the indivual has moved to France, the appropriate local tax centre. (*Centre des Impots*) should be notified. Once registered with the tax authority, residents are required to submit an online declaration each year. Income tax isn't yet deducted at source and each individual is required to make their own declaration.

The tax year runs from 1st January to 31st December and each household receives the tax demand (*avis d'imposition*) a few months after completing the tax return which details the amount to pay and the due date for payment.

INCOME TAX

Income tax is based on the total income of a household. A household consists of married or PACSed couples and their dependents.

An allowance is granted for the *quotient familial* . The allowance system benefits married or PACSed couples with dependent children ie children under 18. Children under 21 can ask to remain within their parents' tax threshold, as can students until age 25. Disabled or infirm children or ascendants can remain within the tax threshold at any age.

Unmarried and non PACSed couples pay more tax. An unmarried couple with a child must declare their child on one or either of the parent's declaration but not both.

There are numerous other allowances which reduce the tax payable and taking these matters into account, large families in France are amongst the lowest taxed in Europe.

CAPTIAL GAINS TAX

Capital gains tax is the tax paid on the profit of sales from certain property in France-most significantly often a second home but can relate to other forms of property.

French residents are exempt from paying tax on any gain from the sale of their main home or on profit from the first sale of a residential property. Properties that have been in the same ownership for thirty years are exempt. In some circumstances sale of a main residence can be exempt for non-residents.

When capital gains is payable the sum due is reduced according to the period of ownership.

The capital gain on taxable property eg. a holiday home is calculated by deducting the purchase price from the sale price. The costs incurred in the sale and the cost of any renovations and improvements to the property can be deducted. Invoices have to be rendered to the seller and contain the relevant siren number etc. of the artisan who carried out the work. The notaire calculates the capital gains payment due and deducts the tax due before transmitting the sale proceeds to the seller.

TVA *taxe sur la valeur ajoutée*

TVA is the French equivalent to VAT. The standard rate is 20 percent and it is applicable to almost everything. There is a reduced rate of 5.5 percent which is applied to most food, agricultural products, books and certain services such as improvement and maintenance works for residential properties. A further reduced rate of 2.1 percent is applied to some press publications and medical drugs.

PENSIONS

Under most double taxation agreements, pensions are only taxed in the country of residence. However, there are some exceptions and under many agreements pensions paid for Government service are taxed only in the country paying the pension.

LOCAL TAXES

Taxe foncière et taxe d'habitation are the taxes attributable to value of property and the number of people living in the property. The owner of the property is liable for the *taxe foncière* and the occupier is liable for the *taxe d'habitation*. An owner-occupier is liable for both taxes.

In the event of a house sale, the seller is liable for the total *taxe foncière* for the year but the amount due is usually apportioned between buyer and seller according to the period of occupation.

Tax varies according to region. Both taxes are based on the notional rental value of the property. Generally the larger the property and the more services available to the property, the higher the tax.

People on low incomes, elderly, widows and widowers, and those in receipt of disability benefits are entitled to reductions.

When the change of ownership of property is registered, the relevant authorities are notified and the tax demands are issued automatically.

It is possible to pay online or by instalment by direct debit.

Further details regarding taxation are available at

www.impots.gouv.fr

It is always advisable to seek advice from a suitably qualified person for detailed advice.

INHERITANCE

Wills made in a country outside of France are unlikely to cover property in France. France has adopted an EU regulation whereby a person resident in France can make a condition in their French will that the law of their national state will be applied to their estate. This is one of the means of bypassing strict French laws regulating inheritance. The option applies to persons originating from another member state of the EU.

A will in France can be made in one of three ways:-

1. A will written in the hand of the donor and signed and dated by them. No witnesses are required but the will must be registered in the register of wills (*fichier de dernieres volontes*)

2. A will is prepared by a notaire, witnessed by two notaires or a notaire and two other witnesses. This type of will is automatically registered in the register of wills.

3. A secret will- this is where the donor writes the will and signs and dates it, the donor then places the will in a sealed envelope and gives it to a notaire in the presence of two witnesses. The notaire stores the will with a note that it is a will entrusted by the donor.

SUCCESSION LAW

Under French law you cannot disinherit your children.

If a deceased person leaves one child, that child will be entitled to half of the estate. If there are two children, each sibling is entitled to claim one third of the estate. If there are three children, they are each entitled to one quarter of the estate. The remaining portion, known as the *quotitent disponible* can be bequeathed to anyone, although the beneficiary is often the spouse or partner of the deceased.

In the absence of a will there is little provision for a surviving spouse or partner under French law.

In situations where a surviving spouse or partner has not inherited the matrimonial property they are entitled to continue to reside in the property for one year following the death or their spouse or partner.

INHERITANCE TAX

The liability for inheritance tax depends on the residence of the deceased. If the deceased was resident in France, the worldwide assets of the deceased are liable to French inheritance tax, for non-residents only property owned in France will be liable to French inheritance tax. There is no tax for beneficiaries who are married or PACSed to the deceased. There are tax free allowances for children. Any benefit above the allowances is taxed on a scale between 5% and 40%.

For inheritances from more distant relatives the allowances are lower and the tax rates higher.

WEALTH TAX

Wealth tax is payable by each individual or couple, if taxed together, with an annual income in excess of 750 000€. It is assessed on the first day of the fiscal year and is payable the following year. There are certain exemptions. French residents are taxable on their worldwide assets. Persons domiciled elsewhere with property in France are taxed only on their property in France.

OWNERSHIP *en indivision*

Usually a property purchased in France will be purchased en division if there is more than one purchaser. This means that when one of the purchasers dies, the deceased person's interest in the property is not passed to the surviving owners but to the deceased surviving children.

CLAUSE TONTINE

It is possible to insist on purchase of property that a *clause tontine* is inserted in the title deed. This means that, on the death of the first purchaser, the deceased's title passes to the remaining owners.

Inheritance tax is payable on the deceased person's share of the property on the first person's death.

MATRIMONIAL REGIME

Couples married in France choose whether to sign a marriage contract or not. This determines how their property will be dealt with on death.

Communauté universelle –On the death of the first spouse, all the property of the marriage is owned by the survivor.

If this regime has not been adopted couples are deemed to have adopted the

Regime of separation of goods- On the death of the first spouse, the usual inheritance laws apply.

A couple can amend this regime by inserting a '*clause d'attribution de communauté au conjoint survivant*' which allows all shared property to pass to the surviving spouse on the first death, and which also defers and French inheritance due until the second death. All that is payable on the first death is a registration fee.

A couple can change regime once they have been married or have had their existing regime for two years. The change must be 'in the interest of the family,' and must be done through the court system.

LIFETIME GIFTS

Under French law if you survive a donation by ten years there is no inheritance payable. Therefore, if you make a gift of your French heritable property, if you survive the donation by ten years, the property gifted will not form part of your estate for which inheritance tax is payable.

SOCIETE CIVILE IMMOBILIERE

A SCI is a company set up to manage property. This is a useful means of property ownership especially if there are non-family owners or if the family situation is complex.

Members of the SCI own shares in the SCI as opposed to the heritable property or real estate. The shares in the company are then governed by the inheritance law applicable to the members of the SCI and are not bound by French inheritance law, as is all heritable property or real estate.

The SCI must have a registered address (usually the address of the property) keep accounts and hold an annual general meeting on French soil.

Members of the SCI can freely give shares to their children or partners during their lifetime to avoid inheritance liability (ten year rule applies). Transfers of a property can occur quickly as it is the shares which transfer. The property remains in the ownership of the SCI.

LES UNIONS LIBRES /PACS

Since 1999, same-sex and different-sex couples can enter into a *Pacte Civil de Solidarité*. This is an agreement between two people. Partners register their PACS at the local court.

A PACS is dissolved by informing the authorities. Once the authorities have been informed the PACS is dissolved after three months.

4. RESIDENCE AND EMPLOYMENT

"choose a job you love, and you will never have to work a day in your life" Confucius

Non EU residents can apply for one of two types of visa to visit France. Residents of EU member states are entitled to free movement between countries.

1. Tourist visa- for short stays under three months. This visa may have to be applied for in the applicant's country of origin. After the maximum period of three months the applicant should leave France and not return for at least another three months.
2. *Visa de long sejour*- visa for over three months. The applicant must apply for the visa at the French Embassy in their country of residence.

FRENCH CITIZENSHIP OR PERMANENT RESIDENCE

After living in France for five years – or less, if the applicant is married to, or the parent of a French national, – it is possible for the applicant to apply for either French citizenship or French permanent residence.

Whether French citizenship or French permanent residence is chosen, both options allow the applicant to continue living in France long-term, although some important differences exist between the two.

A French permanent residence permit allows the applicant to stay in France for ten years and, as it's renewable, theoretically the applicant could live in France indefinitely with this status. Whilst this status grants the applicant many of the same rights as French citizens (e.g. in education, at work, in healthcare), it does not grant all rights, for example, there is no entitlement to vote in elections or hold public office.

A French citizen is also a citizen of the European Union (EU), and holds the same entitlement to freedom of movement throughout EU member states.

A 'continuous' stay in France for a number of years is a requirement for a citizenship application. The 'continuous' stay can be void if the applicant leaves France for more than six consecutive months out of a total of ten months, although exceptions exist in certain cases.

Once an applicant has lived in France for five continuous years, the applicant may apply for a *carte de résidence*, which is a renewable permanent residence permit which allows the applicant to live in France for up to ten years. Whether or not the application is granted will depend on the applicant's personal circumstances, such as the reason for the continued stay, employment and financial stability, how well the applicant has is integrated into French society and the applicant's language ability.

The applicant loses the right to permanent residence if the applicant leaves France for more than two consecutive years.

EU/EEA/Swiss citizens

EU/EEA/Swiss citizens who have been resident in France for five or more continuous years have the option to apply for permanent residence without the need to prove income or employment.

EU/EEA/Swiss nationals are no longer obliged to hold this permit but without it they cannot qualify for state services, such as housing financial aid.

Non-EU/EEA/Swiss nationals can apply for permanent residence after five years,

Exemptions for family members or partners

The five-year residency requirement is reduced to three years if the applicant is joining a family member who already has permanent residence, or if the applicant is the parent of a child with French nationality with temporary residence. Anyone who meets the conditions of French citizenship via birth also has right to permanent residence.

If the applicant has been married to a French national for more than three years, the applicant can apply for permanent residence immediately, even if the applicant has not lived in France during the marriage. If the applicant has been married for less than three years, then the applicant can apply after three years of holding a *carte de séjour* (residence permit).

Application for French permanent residence

Application for either French citizenship or permanent residence can be made at the local French *préfecture* (town hall). Application forms and details of the supporting documentation required are available online. Necessary documentation may include documents proving residence in France, an employment contract, bank statements, birth or marriage certificates and medical certificate.

Depending on which conditions are met, an applicant can consider either French permanent residency or EU long-term residence, the latter providing additional benefits to moving around and living in other EU members states.

Application to become a French citizen

An applicant can apply to become a French citizen with all the accompanying rights (like voting in French elections) through either naturalisation, marriage or birth (whether born in France or born to a French parent while abroad). The applicant must be over eighteen and be resident in France.

Naturalisation

An applicant can apply to become a naturalised French citizen if-

They have been living in France for five continuous years (less under certain circumstances, such as having studied in a French university, in which case it's two years);

can prove integration into the French community by speaking French and having a knowledge of French culture and society and the rights and duties of French citizens.

If the applicant is obtaining French citizenship through naturalisation or marriage, the applicant must sign the Reception and Integration Contract (CAI). This form is valid for twelve months, after which the applicant will be evaluated to see whether they have met the requirements of the CAI, for example, have become sufficiently proficient in French or taken a civics class.

Marriage

An applicant can become a French citizen after four years of marriage to a French citizen, as long as:

They are still married to each other;

The applicant's spouse retains his/her French citizenship; and

The applicant can prove a good knowledge of the French language.

The time requirement is increased to five years in certain cases, for example, if the applicant cannot prove continuous residence in France with their spouse for at least three years since the wedding.

If the applicant was married out with France, before acquiring citizenship the marriage must be registered in the French civil registry.

Birth

If the applicant was born in France or to a French parent the applicant is entitled to apply for citizenship.

Children born to foreign citizens on French soil can claim French citizenship on their 16th birthday and may be granted full citizenship at eighteen years of age provided France has been their main residence for five consecutive years after the age of eleven.

Children may acquire French citizenship at eighteen years of age if they have lived in France since the age of six, attended a French school and have a sibling who has obtained French citizenship.

A foreign parent of a child aged at least thirteen years of age and resident in France since eight years of age, may claim French citizenship on behalf of the child in front of a magistrate. If one parent has French citizenship and has lived in France for more than five years, a minor can also be naturalised.

An applicant, not born in France, but born to a French parent, may apply for a *demande de attribution* at the local *mairie*.

Foster and adopted children may also claim French citizenship if their guardian is a French citizen.

Exceptions to the residence requirement for French citizenship

An applicant may apply immediately for French citizenship, without the five year waiting period, if the applicant has:

1. served in the French military;

2. qualifies as a refugee;

3. contributed 'exceptional services' to France;

4. have come from a country where French is the official language and have attended a Francophone school for a minimum of five years.

If a foreign-born person is the child of a French parent, citizenship may be obtained as of right by making a petition for a French nationality certificate. The applicant is not required to live in France to make this application.

An application for citizenship is made at the applicant's local prefecture. The applicant requires to submit a declaration request (*demande d'acquisition par declaration*) with copies of the following, if applicable:

Two copies of the application form, signed and dated;

Copies of ID of both the applicant and spouse;

Proof of address with the applicant's name;

Birth certificate (with certified translation if not in French);

Marriage certificate;

Attestation sur l'honneur des 2 époux, a document, which both spouses need to sign in person at the *préfecture* or consulate;

Evidence of the relationship or married life such as birth certificates of the spouses' children, a mortgage contract, joint tax notice, property deeds or shared bank account;

Proof of the spouse being a French citizen at the time of marriage;

Proof that the applicant has acquired a sufficient knowledge of the French language, such as a French language diploma or certificate.;

Evidence that the applicant does not have a criminal record, for example, a criminal record certificate from the applicant's country of residence for the previous ten years;

Proof of employment or financial support.

The application is assessed by the police, mayor's office and various other governmental departments, and the applicant may be interviewed by the police. The process can take up to two years.

If successful, the applicant will become a French citizen in a naturalisation ceremony, and will be given a French national ID card and a French passport. Any unmarried dependents automatically become French if they live with the applicant and are included in the naturalisation decree.

RETIREMENT

Retirement in France is relatively straightforward.

The applicant requests a *visa de long sejour-retraite* at the French Consulate. The supporting documentation regarding ID and status are supplied together with proof of income to demonstrate that the applicant can support themselves and has appropriate health insurance cover.

EU NATIONALS

Brexit: At present, the UK is still part of the European Union so free movement applies and UK nationals together with other nationals of the remaining countries in the EU are free to move to France. At present British citizens are entitled to freedom of movement within the European Union. No changes will be made to this entitlement until the UK's exit from the European Union is negotiated or the 28th March 2019 when the two year time limit for negotiations following the trigger of Article 50 is reached.

France at present allows dual citizenship so British citizens can apply for permanent residence or citizenship should they wish.

NON EU NATIONALS

Non-EU nationals are permitted to enter and remain in France for up to one month if they are in possession of a ten year passport.

Non-EU nationals must be in possession of a work permit obtained before they entered France in order to undertake any type of work.

Non-EU nationals must apply for a visa if they intend to stay in France for over a month.

SHORT STAY WORK VISAS

The applicant's employer should issue a contract of employment. The applicant completes a short stay visa application and lodges it with a photograph, a valid passport, and proof of health insurance with world-wide cover.

LONG STAY WORK VISAS

NON EU nationals require to obtain a work contract approved by *the Direction Départmentale du Travail, de l'Emploi et de la Formation Professionnelle* and a long stay visa before arriving in France. The employer in France applies for the work permit to the Office des Migrations Internationals. Once the hiring of the non EU national is approved the OMI transfers the dossier to the French Consulate. The applicant then submits a passport, (valid with two passport sized photographs and the visa fee)

The applicant then applies for a *carte de sejour* at their local *préfecture* or *mairie* within a week of arrival.

The documents required to accompany the application are a valid passport, birth certificate, marriage certificate if applicable, proof of residence, four passport type photographs, services bill, proof of financial resources-if not working.

If the applicant is taking up employment a contract of employment will be required.

Retired applicants require to produce evidence of their state pension, students require to submit proof of their registration at a French educational establishment.

The *carte de sejour* is generally issued in a few weeks. If the applicant plans to be resident in France for a fixed period under five years, the carte will be issued for the period of the stay only. If the applicant is seeking to remain in France permanently the *carte* will be issued for a period of five years and can be renewed. Residency rights granted with the carte can be extended to the applicant's spouse, dependent descendants under 21 and dependent ascendants.

Further information

www.service-public.fr

www.ofii.fr

SOCIAL SECURITY

The French Social Security System is known as *Le Secu*.
Contributions are collected by URSAFF (*Union de Recouvrement des Cotisations de sécurité sociale et d'allocations familiales)*.
URSAFF passes the funds to the ACOSS (*Agence centrale des organismes de sécurité sociale)* which distributes benefits.

When a new employee is hired, the employer files a declaration *unique d'embauche* with www.due.fr and this automatically registers the employee for social security contributions which are then deducted automatically from their salary each month. The employee must have a French social security number.

Family income support is paid through CAF (*Caisse d'allocations familiales)*

www.caf.fr

A self-employed person pays social security contributions for health care, family allowances, invalidity, pension and death. They do not pay contributions for unemployment insurance, so are not able to receive state benefits under the system of unemployment cover. It is possible to obtain cover under private insurance, but it is expensive to do so.

When a business is registered the *Centre de Formalitiés* will notify the various social security agencies who will, in turn, communicate with the self-employed person about their entitlements and the contributions they require to make.

HEALTHCARE

Healthcare in France operates under the provision of a *carte vitale*.

Any full time resident in France can obtain a *carte vitale*. It is necessary to prove full time residence. This usually requires production of utility bills, production of lease agreement for residence or proof of property purchase. Proof of employment, if applicable is also required. If the applicant is unemployed they will require to pay the necessary, fee or *cotisation* in order to obtain a *carte vitale*. The fee is paid annually and is income based.

The *carte vitale* does not provide complete cover. One hundred percent cover is provided for the most serious of illnesses and diseases. Almost all other health cover is provided for at a rate of seventy percent of the total cost. The remainder due is paid by the individual or their top up medical insurance if they have taken up private top up cover in the form of a *mutuelle*.

UK retirees in France are automatically entitled to provision of a *carte vitale* and application is made to the International Pension Centre, Tyneview Park, Newcastle upon Tyne NE98 1BA

EU CITIZENS

EU citizens have entitlement to a European Health Insurance Card, which provides entitlement to health care, either free or at a reduced rate within the EU and Switzerland.

The European Health Insurance Card is valid for between three and five years and provides the same health cover that would be available to a citizen of the country being visited.

Further information

www.dh.gov.uk

5. DRIVING IN FRANCE

"Europeans, like some Americans, drive on the right side of the road, except in England, where they drive on both sides of the road, Italy where they drive on the sidewalk; and France, where if necessary, they will follow you right into the hotel lobby."

Dave Barry

OBTAINING A FRENCH DRIVING LICENCE

EU members can drive on their member state licence until it expires.

Anyone committing a driving offence which leads to a loss of points or withdrawal of their licence will require to exchange their licence for a French one.

Non-EU members are entitled to drive on their foreign licenses for up to a year of obtaining a *carte de sejour*. Then they must obtain a French license. If French licences are recognised in the country of grant of the original licence, the original licence can be exchanged for a French one at the local prefecture. If not, the applicant requires to take a French driving test or drive a vehicle which does not require a license.

SANS PERMIS-VEHICHLES NOT REQUIRING A LICENSE

Microcars or *voitures sans permis* have a maximum of two seats and an engine size of up to 50 cc for petrol engines, 1kw for electric cars or 4kw for diesel vehicles and a maximum speed of 45km/h

These vehicles have grown in popularity in isolated rural areas where being able to drive is essential.

DRIVING REGULATIONS

France has a few anomalies so here are a few things to watch out for

1. A warning triangle and warning florescent jacket which conform to EU standards, must be carried in every car being driven in France.

2. Drive on the right side of the road

3. Pedestrians have priority over cars at pedestrian crossings. The pedestrian should signal clearly their intention to cross- e.g. with a hand signal. If the vehicle is closer than 50m at the time of signal the vehicle is not obliged to stop.

4. *Priorité a droite*- indicated by a black X on a white background in a red triangle. Cars from the right have priority. This means, unless drivers are at a stop sign, traffic lights or a roundabout, the driver should give priority to motorists coming on to the road from the right.

5. Vehicles require to have a *controle technique* after four years. This has been less stringent than the UK equivalent MOT however much more stringent tests are being introduced in 2018. The CT requires to be renewed every two years.

6. Speed limits. Limits are 130km/h on motorways, this is reduced to 100km/h in rain or snow. Regional roads have a limit of 90km/h, and built up areas 50km/h.

7. Stop signs mean stop. You must stop even if there is no other traffic.

8 Drivers must be over 18 to legally drive in France on a foreign license.

9. It is compulsory for drivers to carry their driving documents in their car. These include driving license, vehicle insurance, vehicle registration (*carte grise*) MOT certificate (*controle technique*), accident form- available from your insurance company or local *mairie* to be completed on site in the event of an accident and signed by any drivers involved.

10. Children under ten years of age are obliged to sit in the back seat of any vehicle and wear a seat belt.

My favourite sign is of course the one featured on the cover of this guide. In French the undernote is *jus du raisin*. This sign can be seen in wine growing areas during harvesting when the roads may be awash with grape juice! Another sign to look out for is one warning of frogs crossing the road.

REGISTRATION OF A VEHICLE

Purchase of a new vehicle.

The dealer will do all the necessary paperwork and issue the necessary *carte grise*, which is the log book equivalent.

Purchase of a second hand vehicle.

Generally second hand car's are much cheaper in the UK and Belgium than in France.

The *carte grise* stipulates the registration number for the vehicle and enables the purchase of new registration plates. In France the registration number includes the appropriate department number and therefore a change of department for a vehicle necessitates a change of registration number.

Importing a vehicle.

Complete a *demande de certificate d'immatriculation* at the motor registration office at your *prefecture* or *sous-prefecture*. This can also be done online –surprisingly easy, or through a designated service provider for a fee.

Supporting documentation required.

1. Vehicles from non EU states require a certificate 846A from the customs services office- *le service des douanes* to demonstrate that French customs requirements have been met.

2. *Controle technique* All cars over four years old have to pass a controle technique before they can be registered. The *controle technique* is a road worthiness test like an UK MOT, and applies to vehicles with a gross weight not exceeding 3.5 tonnes. The *controle technique* must dated within six months. A *controle technique* from another EU member state if performed within six months should also be acceptable.

3. Certificate of conformity, if required from the vehicle manufacturer or a certified representative. This certifies

that the vehicle is of a recognised type in France.

4. Proof of identity- passport

5. Proof of residence-recent service bill

6 Proof of purchase

7 If importing the vehicle-customs clearance certificate

8. Fee- a tax is payable, which is calculated according to the engine power of the vehicle

CLASSIC CARS

Vehicles over 25 years of age may be subject to exceptions, further details can be obtained from the *Federation Francaise des Vehicules d'Epoque.*

Purchase of a vehicle within France.

If the vehicle is purchased within France, the vendor should have obtained a *controle technique* dated within six months of the date of sale if the vehicle is more than four years old. The vendor should supply the current *carte grise* and a bill of sale. The seller marks on the *carte grise* the words ' *vendu le* ' and the date and signs it. He should produce a certificate certifying the car is not subject to a loan. Then the *declaration de cession* is completed. This is a form completed in triplicate and signed by buyer and seller. The buyer and seller each keep a copy and the third copy should be transmitted to the prefecture for registration within two weeks.

A fresh *carte grise* is then issued to the purchaser.

The paperwork can again be completed online, or through a designated service provider for a fee.

LEARNING TO DRIVE IN FRANCE

MOPEDS AND MOTORCYCLES

Teenagers can drive a moped from age 14 if the engine capacity is below 50cc - maximum speed of 45kph. Mopeds must be registered and insured and riders without a full driving license must take a test which consists of a theory paper and five hours of practical training- 4.5 hours of which must be on a public road with a driving school. A metal plate with the owners name must be attached to the handlebars of the moped. Mopeds are not permitted on motorways and riders must use cycle paths when provided.

Sixteen year olds cans ride a motorcycle of up to 125cc. They require to obtain a license A1. There is a theory test ASSR2 which can be taken at school. Eighteen year olds can begin training for a full motorcycle license but cannot drive a motorbike over 34hp until age twenty one.

The holder of a vehicle licence is entitled to ride a motorcycle up to 125 hp provided that the holder has held the licence for a minimum of two years. If the vehicle licence has been held for more than five years without a motorcycle having been driven the holder should retake the theory test.

CARS

ACCOMPANIED DRIVER SCHEME

A scheme allowing teenagers from the age of fifteen years to learn to drive, by driving a minimum of 3000 kms with a supervising adult.

Before beginning driving the learner must complete an initial practical course at a driving school and pass the theory test.

The supervising adult must be over twenty eight and have held a clean driving licence for at least three years. The supervising driver is obliged to observe drink drive laws. The learner drives the 3000kms during a period between one and three years. The learner requires to keep a record of routes –distance and road conditions. During this period the learner and the supervising adult are required to attend two theory and practice sessions at a driving school. The learner must observe reduced speed limits-80kph on ordinary roads and 110 kph on dual carriageways.

Accompanied driver vehicles have a white sticker with the outline of two heads in black, the small head is smiling with a steering wheel with the larger head alongside.

DRIVING LESSONS AND TEST

The alternative method to learn to drive is to have lessons and sit a test. Applicants must be at least 17 years of age and resident in France at the time the test is taken.. Learners must have at least twenty lessons from a driving instructor.

The applicant is required to sit a theory test before commencing.

After obtaining a driving licence, the driver has a restricted amount of points-ie 6.

Licences in France start with twelve points and points are deducted as penalties for offences.

New drivers vehicles must display a red letter A on a white sticker and new drivers during the three year probationary period have a reduced speed limit which they must observe- 10kmph lower than the speed limit applicable to other drivers.

Probationary drivers have a lower limit of alcohol/blood than is allowed for more experienced drivers.

DRINK DRIVING REGULATIONS

It is an offence in France to drive with an alcohol/blood over 0.5mg/ml per litre of blood.

Where the blood /alcohol level is between 0.5mg/ml and 0.8mg/ml per litre the fine is 135€ with 6 penalty points and the possibility of disqualification.

Where the blood/alcohol level is over 0.8mg/ml per litre the case will be referred to court for disposal. A period of up to three years imprisonment can be imposed, a fine of up to 4500€ , and 6 penalty points although disqualification for up to three years is more likely.
Police can impose a period of disqualification of up to 6 months pending the case calling before a court for disposal.

The same penalties apply for driving whilst under the influence of drugs.

A supervising driver under the accompanied driver scheme would be liable to the same penalties as if they had been driving the vehicle themselves.

Driving licence points can be removed by letter, or following a court appearance depending on the offence. If the driver has been driving on a foreign licence they may have to transfer their licence to a French one, so that the requisite points can be removed.

RECUPERATION OF POINTS

Points can be recuperated through –

1.Passage of time. The period at which the points are returned depends on the number of points originally imposed and whether the driver was driving during the probationary period.

2.Attending a *stage*. Drivers who are still entitled to drive but are anxious about the lack of points on their licence can choose to attend a course after which they are accredited points on their licence.

6. TAKING PETS TO FRANCE

"better to be the head of a dog than the tail of a lion"

DOGS AND CATS

Dogs and Cats are allowed to travel between the UK and France, without quarantine if they are certified by the Pet Travel Scheme (Pets)

PETS TRAVEL SCHEME

This scheme covers the UK, European countries and other countries including USA and Canada. A maximum of three cats or dogs per person can be brought into France. Of the three animal quota only one can be a puppy. The minimum age of each animal is three months.

The pet can leave the UK from anywhere, by any means of transport but can only return to the UK on an authorised route with an approved transport company.

Entry points to the UK

Ports- Dover, Harwich, Hull, Portsmouth, Southhampton.

Airports –Birmingham, Heathrow, Leeds, Manchester, Glasgow,Edinburgh, Prestwick

Rail- Eurotunnel

QUALIFYING FOR PETS

The animal must be –

1. Fitted with a microchip

2. Vaccinated against rabies
3. Blood tested to show the vaccination has worked

A Local Veterinary Inspector (LVI) issues a certificate-PETS 1-identifying the animal and confirming the successful vaccination against rabies. The certificate specifies a period of validity and when a booster rabies vaccination will be required.

PETS 2

This is a certificate enabling the animal return to the country of origin. A vet confirms that the animal has been treated against tapeworm and ticks. The certificate is issued by a vet in a foreign country, between 24 hours and 48 hours before the animal returns to the country of origin, unless the animal has been on a day trip abroad in which case it can be completed by a vet in the country of origin.

PETS 3

This is a certificate whereby the owner confirms that the animal has not travelled to a country out with the PET Travel Scheme

PETS 5

Some countries in PETS request an export health certificate for the animal's entry. France requires a document called a 'Export of a pet dog or cat to France in accordance with the Pet Travel Scheme. This is a PETS 5 which is a copy of the PETS 1, but translated into French.

The PETS 5 can be obtained at the same time as the PET 1. If you already have a current PETS 1 you can obtain a PETS 5 from any LVI on production of the valid PETS 1. The certificate is valid from the date of signature.

RETURNING TO THE UK

Unless the animal has been on a day trip outside the UK, the animal can only re-enter the UK at least six months after the date of its blood test. The six month period runs from the date the blood sample was taken, not the date of the result of the test analysis. If the owner wants to take the animal back to the UK before the six month period has expired the animal is required to go into quarantine.

The PETS certificate is valid until the next rabies vaccine is due. This will be from one to three years after the date of the original vaccine. If the animal is to become resident in France, a vaccine for only one year is necessary as France has compulsory annual vaccinations.

If the date for the booster vaccination passes without revaccination taking place the process has to start afresh from the beginning.

PETS in France

In order to renew a PETS certificate in France, the animal must have received an annual vaccination against rabies. If there is more than a year gap between rabies vaccinations the vet can refuse to issue a renewal certificate and therefore the process must start afresh.

Dogs and Cats becoming resident in France

If the dog or cat is resident in France for more than three months it becomes resident and must be registered on a national database. The dog or cat must be identified by either a tattoo or suitable microchip.

TAKING A HORSE OR PONY TO FRANCE

All horses and ponies are required to have a passport identifying the animal.

PASSPORTS

Passports are obtained by applying to one of the organisations authorised by DEFRA (Department for Environment, Food and Rural Affairs) to issue passports.

Passports last for the lifetime of the animal. EU legislation stipulates that the passport includes a silhouette of the animal so that it can be identified. This is a drawing showing the markings on the animal or a list of the colourings and markings. A microchip can be used in addition to the silhouette but is not compulsory. The silhouette should be completed by a vet or a suitable person authorised by the society issuing the passport.

The horse or pony will be issued with an UELN –unique equine life number which is marked on the passport.

Export Health Certificate

An export health certificate is required along with the passport to move horses and ponies between EU member states. An examination is carried out by a vet within 48 hours of loading the animal and is signed by a vet on behalf of DEFRA.

The vet must ensure that the animal meets all the necessary health conditions i.e. has been appropriately vaccinated, for export but also that the vehicle or container transporting the animal is suitable for the purpose.

OTHER PETS

If the animal being transported to France does not fall into the PETS scheme and is not a horse or pony, an Export Health Certificate should be obtained.

GRAIN EATING BIRDS

For birds of the Psittacidae family-e.g. parrots, parakeets, etc. – entry is limited to two birds per person. The importer has to declare that they have owned the birds for over six months and undertakes not to sell them in France and to allow the birds be examined by a vetinary inspector. There is an export license for birds going to France which is obtained from DEFRA and is valid for ten years.

Contacts

Department for Environment, Food and Rural Affairs (DEFRA)

www.defra.gov.uk

British Horse Society

www.bhs.org.uk

IFFE –French Horse Federation

www.ffe.com

DOGS

Dogs are not required to wear identification discs as there is no formal licencing system. However all dogs born after 6th January 1999 must have an identifying number. This is in the form of a microchip or tattoo.

The identify numbers are retained by the SPA which is the French Society for the Protection of Animals.

Dogs should be kept on leads in most public parks and gardens.
On public transport pets weighing under 6kg should be carried in an appropriate cage. Larger dogs , if permitted will require a muzzle and lead.

Some dogs –eg pit bull terrier are required to be muzzled in public places.

Additional information
Regulations regarding importation and keeping of pets
www.agriculture.gouv.fr

Importation of exotic pets
www.douane.gouv.fr

7. COURTS AND POLICE

"c'est la fin des haricots" literally the end of the beans used as equivalent to the last straw.

Civil Law

The *Code Civil*, or *Code Napoléon*, (Civil code or Napoleonic code) governs the rights and obligations of citizens, and the laws of property, contract, inheritance and other civil matters. The code incorporates principles of Roman Law and common law which were in existence when the original code was set down in 1804 and is updated regularly.

The *code civil* is divided into two parts:-

The *Droit public*, or Public law, defines the principles of operation of the state and public bodies and is usually applied through public law courts, known as *les Tribunaux administratifs.*

The *Droit privé*, or private law, applies to private individuals and private bodies. The *droit prive* is applied through the judicial courts. The judicial courts are divided into two sections, one deals with civil litigation the other with criminal offences.

Civil litigation concerning private individuals is dealt with by a local court, the *Tribunal d'Instance*, or by a regional or departmental court, the *Tribunal de Grande Instance* (TGI), depending on the importance of the case. Commercial and business law is administered through institutions known as *Tribunaux de commerce*. These are known as "first degree courts".

Appeals are heard in a *Cour d'Appel* or Court of Appeal. There is a fundamental right of appeal in all cases. In exceptional circumstances, judgements of the Appeal Court can be contested at

the highest level, the *Cour de Cassation*, the French
Supreme Court in matters of private law.

Criminal Law

 Everyday offences and petty criminal matters are generally dealt
with either by a *Juge de proximité* (a local magistrate) or a
Tribunal de Police (police court). More serious offences are
referred to the *Tribunal Correctionnel,* the criminal law equivalent
of the TGI. The most serious criminal offences, notably murder
and rape,are referred to a *Cour d'Assises*, or Assize court, where
they are tried by jury.

Public Law

Complaints or litigation concerning public officials in the exercise
of their office are heard in *Tribunaux Administratifs,* or
Administrative Courts. For example, universities can be taken to
court over claimed irregularities in the conduct of exams. Appeals
from the *tribunaux administrative* decisions lie to the *Cour
administratif d'appel*, or Administrative appeals court. The
Supreme Court for public law, is the *Conseil d'Etat,* or Council of
State which can hear appeals from the administrative appeals court.

French courts are presided over by *Juges* (Judges) also known as
Magistrats (magistrates). *Magistrats,* are highly qualified
professionals, almost all of whom have graduated from the
postgraduate School of Magistrature.

Criminal court proceedings can be presided over by a *juge d'instruction*. The judge who is appointed to the case is in charge of preparing the case and deciding whether it should come to court. This system is known as inquisitorial, because it is the responsibility of the judge to direct enquiries to ensure the requisite evidence is before the court.

In court, the judge or judges directs the prosecution and the defence, both of which are usually represented by lawyers, or *avocats*. Juries are only used in assize courts.

If the case goes to appeal, the arguments of the prosecution and the defence are presented by appeals specialists known as *Avoués*.

Legal aid is available and applications can be made through the Maison de Justice, which is usually attached to the *Tribunal d'Instance*.

POLICE

There are four main police forces in France:-

The *police nationale –agents de police* deal with all crime within the jurisdiction of their police station and are under the control of the Interior Ministry.

The *gendarmerie nationale* form part of the army and are under the control of the Ministry of Defence. They deal with serious crime throughout France and are responsible for policing rural areas. They also deal with motorway patrols, air and coastal patrols and air safety.

Compagnie Republicaine de la Securite deal with crowd control and public disturbances.

Police municipale based in towns and cities and deal with petty crime and traffic offences.

The *police municipale* are the only force which are not armed.

Any police officer can stop any person and demand to see identification. They can stop any vehicle and demand to see driving license and insurance documents together with the *carte grise*. Anyone unable to produce the requisite documents can be arrested.

Anyone arrested is obliged to provide their name, age and permanent address. The police can detain a suspect for up to 24 hours in custody. A suspect is entitled to a meeting with a lawyer within three hours of their detention. After detaining a suspect for 24 hours, the police require the authority of a judge to continue to detain the suspect. If the alleged offense involves state security, two further extensions of 48 hours may be granted.

8 FRENCH CUSTOMS

"I cannot prevent the French from being French"

Charles de Gaulle

THE BISE

The conundrum of the *bise*. When to kiss and when not to kiss. There is no easy answer. Some regions of France kiss once, others twice, some three times or even four. Relatives may kiss up to six times. Either right or left cheek may be kissed first. It is a matter of following the lead of the other person. Often once you become better acquainted with someone they will say '*On fait la bise?*' to request permission to begin using the *bise* as a greeting. The most important thing to remember is that once you have started greeting someone with a *bise,* it is very rude to stop.

BONJOUR

In the rural South-West it is usual to say 'bonjour' on entering small shops, the doctor's etc.

NOISE

It is common for there to be noise restrictions in towns and villages. The restrictions are imposed locally and therefore there are variations. The restrictions prevent use of noisy items like lawn-mowers and generally apply before 8am in the morning and after 7pm in the evening on weekdays and before 8am and after mid-day at weekends.

CHRISTMAS

French advent calendars end on the 24th December. This is
because the French tend to have their Christmas meal on the
evening of the 24th. Adults may still be having their Christmas
meal at midnight on the 24th and can then open their Christmas
presents.

FETE DE ROIS

This is three kings day and is celebrated on the 6th January in
France to mark Epiphany. Bakers sell the *galette de roi,* which is a
traditional round pastry cake with a golden paper crown. The cake
will have hidden inside a *feve* or favour. The person who finds the
favour is chosen as king or queen for the day and gets to wear the
crown.

BONFIRES

Depending on the area of France there are restrictions on when
bonfires can be lit. The local *mairie* will be able to advise on the
restrictions in place.

9. WILDLIFE

"petit a petit l'oiseau fait son nid" little by little the bird makes its nest.

HORNETS

European hornets are the largest European member of the wasp family. The adults are between two and three and half centimetres in length. They are brown with yellow stripes on the abdomen. They are not particularly aggressive unless their nest is under threat and are known as gentle giants in Germany. Hornets live in colonies. The queen hibernates over the winter and starts building a nest in the spring. Popular nest sites include holes in trees, attics, chimneys and wall voids, and occasionally in the ground and exposed sides of buildings. European hornets feed on grasshoppers and other large insects including bees. They also gather sap from plants. They are active at night and are attracted to lights. In late summer, male hornets and fertile females begin to hatch. They mate and the fertile females hibernate over the winter. The males and workers die as winter approaches.

European hornets have a similar venom to common wasps. Anyone allergic to a common wasp sting is therefore likely to be allergic to a hornet sting. A typical hornet can sting between three and five times before it runs out of venom. In the event of an allergic reaction to a sting, urgent medical attention is required. In other circumstances the sting should be removed with a flat object like a credit card or a butter knife. Squeezing the sting can result in more venom being released. After removal of the sting, any tight clothes or jewellery in the area of the sting should be removed. Then an ice pack should be applied. Wiping vinegar on the sting can help.

My first night in our newly purchased house in France is seared in my memory. Not because we had no furniture, but because it was like being an extra in a Killer Bees movie.

I can still see the giant wasps crawling down the mosquito screens over our windows. The darker the night became, the more their numbers increased.

After a virtually sleepless night trying to identify our frightening neighbours on an interminably slow internet connection, we discovered European hornets.

Being from the North of Scotland, these insects were an entirely new and unwelcome experience. I arrived in France with a fear of wasps. After one night I was cured.

Three days of terror followed as my then husband insisted on evicting our unwelcome visitors from their nest in our lounge chimney. That involved keeping a fire going for three days, during one of the hottest Augusts on record, when I was too frightened to open the windows or step out of the house.

Ten years on I have come to terms with life with hornets. I keep a can of hornet spray in the living room and call an appropriate expert to dispose of it, if I find a nest. Some people put out a mixture of beer and jam in plastic bottles hanging in trees to catch the queens when they appear in late spring.

Asian hornets have spread rapidly in France since arriving from Asia in 2005. The queens are up to three centimetres in length and have a dark brown or black, velvety body with a fine yellow band. The last body segment is almost entirely yellow or orange. The hornets usually nest in trees but do sometimes nest in buildings. They rarely nest in wall cavities. They are active during the day until dusk when they cease activity. The Asian hornet feeds on honey bees and other insects.

PROCESSIONARY CATERPILLERS

The moth which develops from the processionary caterpillar lives for a day or more correctly a night. It lays its eggs in summer, usually high up in a pine tree. The young caterpillars make their initial nest, then in the autumn they make larger nests, like giant cobwebs which are clearly visible. The caterpillars spend the winter, in colonies, sometimes of several hundreds, in their nests. The caterpillars are nocturnal, feeding at night on pine needles.

Depending on weather conditions, the caterpillars leave the trees between December and May. They can be seen on the ground, in long nose to tail processions- hence their name- as they search a suitable location to pupate. The caterpillars have orange brown backs with bluish grey bands and bluish grey protrusions in pairs on each body segment. The protrusions have hairs growing from them and it is these hairs which can be dangerous. The hairs contain a highly allergenic protein which, in humans, can cause reactions ranging from mild itching to anaphylactic shock. The hairs are particularly dangerous for dogs who may sniff the caterpillars. If animals come into contact or swallow the caterpillars, severe swelling of the tongue and breathing difficulties may result.

The caterpillars are usually easily visible and generally only present a danger between December and May.

Having read an article explaining how if a nest of processionary caterpillers was found, it should be immediately reported to the local mairie who would then organise deposal of the nest in one of the English language magazines which promote life in France, I was alarmed to discover a nest in our garden. Armed with the article, I set of to the mairie, having practised my pronunciation of the appropriate phrases. Contrary to the information provided in the article, the mairie were completely uninterested in my

discovery, and had no interest whatsoever in arranging removal of
the nest. I helpfully provided my copy of the article which I had
cut from the magazine to the receptionist, but she merely shrugged
and repeated that it was a matter for me to deal with, if I had any
concerns about the nest.

SNAKES

Most varieties of snakes found in France are harmless. There are
four poisonous varieties-these are:-

ASP VIPER-This is a small snake found all over France apart from
the extreme north and north east, it is generally considered the
most venomous. Most snakes are between twenty and thirty
centimetres long with the largest being up to around seventy five
centimetres. The snake is recognisable by its flattened triangular
head. The body can be light grey, brown and various shades of
orange with darker marks forming a distinctive zig zag pattern
down the central back. The snake hunts in early evening or night
and feeds on small mammals. The venom fangs are retracted
except at the moment of biting. Many first defensive bites have
little or no venom injected. The snake hibernates between October
and March.

COMMON ADDER. This is found in the North and East of
France, and the Massif Central. It grows to a maximum of ninety
centimetres. The snake has a flattened head with either a black
mark resembling a letter X or V. Colouration varies according to
region and sex. Most varieties of the snake have backs with a
distinctive zig zag pattern. They hunt mainly at dawn and dusk
feeding on small mammals, birds, amphibians and lizards. The
snake is a good swimmer. It hibernates between October and
March.

ORSINI VIPER. This is found in a small area of the south east of France. It is now endangered. The back is usually grey in colour with a distinctive zig zag marking in black. It is usually under half a metre in length.

MONTPELLIER SNAKE. This is found mostly found in the South of France. It can grow up to 1.8metres. It feeds on lizards, rabbits and small rodents.

Keeping the grass cut around the house discourages snakes. It is prudent to wear wellington boots if walking through long grass.

WILD BOAR

Wild Boar or *sanglier* are found all over France and are probably the most hunted mammal in France as they are much prized for their meat. The wild boars preferred habitation is dense forest and undergrowth. They are mainly nocturnal and usually live in close family groups. Males have large tusks used for digging and defending themselves. Adult males can weigh up to three hundred kilograms. The boars feed on berries, fruit, fungi, grains, root and grass. They also root about in the soil for worms, insects and acorns. The animals are hunted to prevent population growth and are frequently blamed for destruction and damage to crops by farmers. The animals, although powerful are shy and retiring and rarely dangerous unless attacked.

RAGONDIN or COYPU

The coypu is a large member of the rodent family and was introduced to France from South America in the nineteenth century. They are probably most similar to beavers in appearance and grow up to sixty centimetres in body length with a long tail. They have course brown fur and adults weigh up to nine kilograms. They are semi aquatic and live near water. They feed on aquatic plants including the roots, maize and fallen fruits. Breeding takes place at any time of the year and a female can have two or three broods a year. The coypu dig tunnels of around twenty centimetres in diameter and ten metres in length. They can undermine banks of lakes and ditches by tunneling.

I once made the mistake, at a reception of eating coypu pate, it was revolting.

FIRE SALAMANDER

The fire salamander is so called because it was believed they lived in fire. It seems this story originated because they tend to hibernate in damp logs and would emerge if one was thrown on a fire. The salamander is widely distributed across France and has a black body with bright yellow markings. They are active during the evening and night when they search for small insects. They can grow up to thirty centimetres long and usually prefer forest habitats. They have a rubbery skin through which they can exude toxins. As a consequence, touching them should be avoided.

10. HUNTING

'Qui court deux lievres a la fois, n'en prend aucun" – who runs
after two hares at the same time, catches none.

Hunting is, for many in rural France, an integral part of life.

Hunting is regulated by each department according to the needs
and requirements of each department. As a result, the dates of the
hunting season and the animals and birds hunted varies.September
the 11th is a popular start date for the hunting season in the South
of France with other areas often starting the season on either the
18th or the 25th of the month.In order to hunt it is necessary to pay
the applicable fee and obtain a hunting permit. Permits are
available from three days to an annual pass.

Each area has a local hunting group or *chasse*. There are strict
rules regarding the conduct of the *chasse*. Their function is
regulate the wildlife population in their designated area and
prevent over population of certain species.

Landowners can complete a form if they wish to exclude the
chasse from crossing their land. The hunters are forbidden from
crossing fenced land or approaching too closely to domestic
dwellings.

11. WINE

"Burgundy makes you think of silly things, Bordeaux makes you talk of them and Champagne makes you do them. "

Anthelme Brillat-Savarin

Wine is an important part of everyday life in France. More so in the areas, like the South West where the life of a significant part of whole communities may revolve around the production of wine. In these areas, it is wine that governs the rhythm of life. It is therefore worthwhile, if you are not already a wine buff, taking the time to learn at least the basics.

VINES

During the first few years of its life, a vine produces no grapes. Its energy is directed at extending roots deep into the ground. After four or five years the vine begins to produce grapes.

WINE GROWERS CALENDER

January-This is when the pruning begins. In wine growers language, 'they cause the vines to weep.' That is to say that when a vine is pruned, drops of sap, like tear drops, well from the cuts. The pruning process involves removing shoots so that the remaining shoots will increase in size, as will the berries produced from the surviving shoots. This is a skilled task for the grower as this pruning process will affect the yield when the vines are harvested.

February-The pruning process continues and cuttings are taken for future plantations

March-The final pruning takes place before the vine awakens with

Spring. The soil around the vine is ploughed and drawn away from the roots of the vine into the centre of the row.

April-The vines shoots are tied. As the shoots are too delicate to support themselves they are tied onto lengths of wire.

May-The soil around the vines is weeded. The leaves are thinned to ensure better ventilation.

June-The vines bloom. The shoots are trimmed and tied to stakes

July-Bordeaux mixture is sprayed and the final cut of overlong shoots takes place.

August-The grapes grow and ripen in the sunshine. The 'green harvest' takes place when some of the bunches of grapes are removed to allow the remaining grapes develop in size and quality.

September-The harvest or '*vidange*', the highlight of the wine growers year, takes place. Harvesting starts around the middle of the month as soon as the grapes are ripe. Machines are sometimes used, although the grapes are handpicked by the Grand Crus and '*liqureux.*' The *chais*, the rooms where the grapes are vinified and stored are prepared.

October-The winegrower is occupied attending to the vinification.

November-The base of the vines is earthed up as a protection against frost.

December-Pruning may begin.

WINE REGIONS

The wine regions are devided into '*appelations*'-the growing area from which the grape has come.

The principal regions are:-

LOIRE – white wine region following the Loire river in central and western France.

CHAMPAGNE –sparkling white and rose wine from Eastern France. Genuine champagne is produced using grapes only grown in the champagne region, using the traditional method known as *methode champenoise* which is very labour intensive.

BORDEAUX-a wine region around Bordeaux and the Gironde department in South-West France. The region produces both mostly red wines with the most famous wines of the region being red.

ALSACE- situated next to France's border with Germany, produces mainly white, sparkling and rose wines. Unlike most of the other wine producing regions in France, Alsace traditionally does not use oak casks to add spice and richness but rely instead on a balance between ripeness of the grapes and alcohol to develop the flavour.

BURGUNDY OR BOURGOGNE- wine from the Burgundy region in Eastern France. Almost all the grapes in the region are made over to the production of red wine although small amounts of white, rose and sparkling wine are also produced. Burgundy has more appellations than any other region in France. In Burgundy the practise of delineating vineyards by their *terroir*, which literally translated means soil but in relation to wine means the specificity of a particular area, goes back to medieval times, when monasteries played a key role in the development of the Burgundy wine industry.

RHONE-wine region in Southern France situated in the Rhone valley. The Northern Rhone produces red wines from the Syrah grape which for some of the regions wines is blended with white wine grapes and a selection of white wines. The Southern region produces an array of red, white and rose wines.

PROVENCE-situated along the Mediterranean coast in Southern France, this area, although it is the oldest wine producing area in France, is also one of the least well known for wine production. The area focuses on the production of rose.

LANGUEDOC-ROUSSILLON- situated on France's southern coast, this is one of the largest wine producing areas in the world and is responsible for more than a third of France's total wine production.

JURA-region in Eastern France is one of France's smallest wine regions and produces both red and white wines.

SOUTH WEST FRANCE-a variety of red, white and rose wines. It is unusual for wines to be marketed under the name of South West France wines and they tend to market themselves in smaller groups.

The French learn from an early age, which wine is the most suitable to accompany each course. Many French recipes suggest a suitable wine accompaniment. The general rule that red wine goes with red meat and white wine with seafood and poultry is easy to follow.

Once you delve deeper, Sauternes is traditionally drunk with *foie gras.* Pinot noir is excellent with duck or quail. However the best and easiest rule to follow is that champagne is drunk with everything celebratory.

12. LEARNING FRENCH AND EDUCATION

LEARN FRENCH

' *'Never too old, never too bad, never too late, never too sick to start from scratch once again."*

Bikram Choudhury.

Whether moving to France permanently or just spending holiday time there, it is well worth making the effort to learn French. If you do so, you will gain much more out of the time you experience in France.

When I first moved to France I was obliged to pre prepare phrases and read them out on arrival at my destination eg. when I enrolled the children as school. I used to turn white when I received a call from a French number on my mobile because, whilst I was able to say 'bonjour' perfectly, I knew I would have no hope of understanding whatever was said to me.

Ten years on, the French I do speak has a very marked Scottish accent and I am still learning. One day, maybe, I will be able to say I speak French as well as my children who are now fluent and bilingual.

There are a wide variety of courses available from free online to residential immersion courses.

Anyone seeking work can enrol at the local *Pole Emploie*. They may arrange free French lessons, to improve prospects of finding employment.

Watching French television with subtitles is another useful tool.

Joining the local community is an easy way to integrate, meet people and have opportunities to practise the French being learnt. Anyone with school aged children can volunteer to assist with the schools outings and functions. The *mairies* are usually grateful for volunteers whether it is to put up decorations at Christmas or make flowers for the summer fetes.

Making an effort in French usually reaps rewards. Often the French person will want to demonstrate that they can speak better in English than you can in French, in which case, you can have the choice to converse in English or battle away, speaking in French whilst the French person responds in English

Bear in mind, that apparently French people find an English accent sexy-the jury's still out on a Scottish accent- so you might find all sorts of unexpected additional benefits to trying out your French.

At a school meeting about my twelve year old son, in his presence, his delightful French teacher assured me that she was always encouraging my son and his English friend to speak, because she, and the rest of the class found the accent so sexy.

Its fun to learn and making mistakes are all part of the process but to save your blushes here are a few mistakes to avoid.

un tampon - a stamp

le preservative –condom- *and yes, I have discussed my concerns about preservatives in the food in a restaurant.*

je suis chaud- I am sexually turned on

j'ai chaud- I am hot

I will never forget the look on the face of my neighbours' ten year old son when, I remarked to him in passing on a very hot August day – Je suis chaud.

Watch your pronunciation !

le connard – asshole   *le canard* -duck-the bird

quand - when   *con* idiot

le cou – neck   *le cul* arsehole

Putin–Russian president *putain* – shit(as an exclamation) – whore (as a noun)

baisser–to lower or reduce   *baiser* –to have sex   *bisser* –to kiss

boules –balls   *bulles* –fizzy – *order l'eau gazzeuse* –its safer!

If you are using an automatic translate take care that your property with gite does not become a property complete with idiot!

VERLAN

Once you have mastered French, you can start on Verlan.

Verlan is a form of slang common in the French language. It is formed by switching or inverting the order in which syllables from the original word appear.

Some verlan words have become so common they have become included in French dictionaries. An example is la femme which in inverted form becomes la meuf.

Once you are ready to start learning, check out :-
en.m.wiktionary.org

GUESTURES

Gestures are as much a form of communication in French as language.

The shrug- everyone is familiar with the Gaullic shrug which has hundreds of meanings from-I don't know to I don't care.

Drunk- twisting one fist around the nose is an indication that someone has had way to much to drink.

Finished- crossing the forearms in front of the body indicates the end.

Lets get out of here- chopping the top of one hand down on the wrist of the other hand is a sign to get out of the situation-fast.

That's a lie- running a finger over the eyelid and down the cheek indicates that the person does not believe what they are being told.

It's easy-placing two fingers towards the nostril.

Bad news- waving one hand up and down.

EDUCATION

Registration.

To enroll your child in a French school you need to –

1. enroll your child at the *mairie* in order to obtain a registration certificate.

2. your *livret de famille*. This is a booklet issued at time of marriage to couples married in France. Any children of the marriage are then recorded in the book. If you weren't married in France you won't have one and will be obliged to produce your child's passports and the parent(s) passports and marriage certificate if applicable, and the child's birth certificate.

3. proof from your doctor that your child is up to date with vaccinations or an exemption certificate.

Once the school authority has the documentation, the child should be enrolled.

Religion and State are separated in France. My first Christmas school play in France involved watching angelic five year olds portray burning down the chapel, having already burnt down their homes and the school–to demonstrate the appropriate number to call for the fire brigade.

Formal compulsory education in France begins at age six. Nursery places begin from age three and can be for a half day or full school day depending on availability. Children must be nappy free to attend nursery. They are expected to sleep after lunch. – *My second youngest child's place was quickly restricted to mornings only, when she refused to snooze on the camp beds provided and had to be chased around the dimmed class room where the other children, more accustomed to an afternoon sieste, were trying to sleep.*

Unless an exception has been made, your child is not allowed to take food into a French school. They have to have the school meal for lunch-usually three courses- or return home for lunch. If they stay for the *garderie* or after school club, they are permitted to take a *gouter* or snack.

When my second youngest child started nursery, I carefully packed in her school bag all the things I would have supplied in the UK, an apple, a carton of juice, a little sandwich. The teacher aware that I was new to the area indulged me for the first two days. On the third, she opened my daughter's school bag and handed back to me all the items I had packed. She politely explained that it was 'interdict 'to bring food into the school and I could be assured that my daughter would eat her lunch at twelve o'clock because she would be hungry.

Ecole maternelle-nursery school.

The objective is for the child to learn how to deal with social situations and become more independent.

Age class

3-4 *petite section*   PS

4-5 *moyenne section* MS

5-6 *grand section*   GS

Ecole Primaire

The Ministry of Education defines the purpose of primary school-

"to ensure the acquisition of the basic tools of knowledge: oral and written expression, reading and arithmetic. It stimulates the development of the intelligence, artistic sensibility, manual and physical skills and sporting abilities. It provides a grounding in the plastic and musical arts, and, in conjunction with the family, undertakes the child's moral and civil education."

The state is obliged to make schooling available for your child in the commune where you live. The school week is generally Monday to Friday with a half day on Wednesday. Generally speaking low cost or free childcare is available, before and after school, from around 8am to 6pm during week days for working parents. In 2015 primary schools introduced additional activities and sport as options included in the school curriculum. Prior to that sports had been regarded as an extra-curricular activity to be arranged by parents on a Wednesday afternoon when there is usually no school.

Children are expected to attain certain minimum standards before they are allowed to progress into the next class. If they do not attain the level desired, the school can recommend they *redouble* or repeat a year. If your child is having difficulty as school or has missed a lot of school in a year, this can result in having to repeat a year, perhaps several times;

Passing into the next school year is therefore considered as something to be celebrated. This is evidenced by *la rentree.*

On the first day back at school, at the beginning of September, after the two month summer holiday, traditionally parents gather, smartly dressed, with their children, and wait for their child's name to be called out and formally invited to enter their new class. The pupils line up and then are led, by their teacher, to the sound of applause from proud parents, into the new class to begin the educational year.

For my first rentree I was quite proud of having got three reluctant children to the school gate before nine a.m. was horrified to find I was expected to wait in my make up less state wearing joggies and trainers to watch my children enter class.

The French have mastered the art of discussion and negotiation, therefore allow entire evenings for school meetings or have an exit strategy. The schools are always looking for volunteers to help at fetes and to provide the number of personnel required for school trips. It is an excellent opportunity to integrate into your local community and to get to know people. *I have some friends who have assisted at local schools and nursery's by reading English to the classes.*

école primaire-primary school

 age class

6-7 *cours preparotoire*   CP

7-8 *cours elementaire première*   CE1

8-9 *cours elementaire deuxième anée* CE2

9-10 *cours moyen première année*   CM1

10-11 *cours moyen deuxième année* CM2

Secondary schools, like the primary maternelles are strictly gated with entry systems. If your child leaves the school premises for any reason they require to have a signed parental authorisation. Students have a complex timetable and a vast array of books, jotters and folders to manage. All part of the learning process,which is required to deal with the administrative requirements which form an integral part of life in France.

Secondary education is divided into two phases. College is preparation for the brivet at the end of troisième and lycée for the baccalauréat.

College is the first stage of secondary education. Students begin learning a foreign language, usually English in *sixième* and a second language in *quatrième*. During *quatrième* students begin to receive careers advice about their future education choices.

Age	Class	
11-12	*sixième*	*6ème*
12-13	*cinqième*	*5ème*
13-14	*quatrième*	*4ème*
14-15	*troisième*	*3ème*

Lycee provides a three year course of further education for students between the ages of fifteen and eighteen. Pupils are prepared for the *baccalauréat* (colloquially known as le bac). The *baccalauréat* can lead to higher education studies or directly to professional life.

Students require to make a choice between a bac pro- technical or vocational option:-

a *bac general* – subjects include literature, economics, social sciences, science, medical

a *bac technologique*-subjects include science and tertiary technologies, industrial technologies and laboratory technologies.

Age   Class

15-16 *second*

16-17 *premiere*

17-18 *terminale*

The *lycée* of choice, if your child has a specific course they wish to study, may be some distance from your place of residence. Many *lycées* have residential options where the student is an intern from Monday morning to Friday evening. Students are strictly supervised and are required to follow strict timetables during the period of their internship.

International Schools.

International schools offer a curriculum which is wholly or partly in English. There are also bilingual schools.

ELSA English language Schools Association

link**http://www.elsa-france.org/** Home Schooling

 Home schooling has been legal, in France since 1998. There are requirements which need to be met which follow closely the requirements of the French curriculum. Annual registration is compulsory, and usually there is an annual visit from the school inspector and a bi-annual visit from the maire.
linkhttp://www.education.gouv.fr/bo/1999/hs3/som.htm

Private Education

Private schools are relatively inexpensive and offer an affordable alternative to the state system.

UNIVERSITY

The French Education System operates under the principal that education should be open to all, therefore university is relatively inexpensive.

GRANDE ECOLES

The largest groups of *grande écoles* are schools of engineering and management studies although there are *grande écoles* for other subjects including veterinary studies. The *grande écoles* are the elite of the French education system and are highly selective. A degree from a *grande école* is equivalent to a European master. Many of the grande école programs are taught in English.

Entrance to a *grande école* may require the applicant to pass an entry exam which may require one or two years study in a preparatory class.

Contacts

link www.education.gouv.fr

 private schools

link www.cide.fr

When I moved to France my children were aged eleven months, three years, eight years and nine years. All, except my youngest who had already lived in France for two years before he started at school had some difficulty, in varying degrees to adjusting and integrating into their new schools.

None of them 'just soaked up the language like sponges.' They weren't all fluent in French within a matter of months. They all undoubtedly had some very difficult experiences to get through.

Having said that, years on it is an experience which they have all to some degree or another benefited from.

As a general rule, the older a child is, the more difficult it will be to integrate into a different school system teaching in a foreign language. Once your child has reached secondary school age, unless you have access to one of the English speaking schools or your child has a particular aptitude for learning French, you may have to put of your French dream for a few years.

Emily

Hello, I am one of Eilidh's children. I moved here when I was three old and I would have to say I learned the French language. It didn't take too long. I'm not going to lie, the school system is very different. I am now in 4iéme. It's getting really difficult, but I'll make it.

13. LA MARSEILLAISE

La Marseillaise is the national anthem of France. If you want to fit in with the French you need to learn at least the first verse and chorus. The song was written in 1792 by Claude Joseph Rouget de Lisle in Strasbourg after the declaration of war by France against Austria, and was originally titled "Chant de guerre pour l'Armée du Rhin" ("War Song for the Rhine Army").

The Marseillaise was a revolutionary song. A patriotic call to inspire all citizens to rise, take up arms and fight against tyranny and foreign invasion. The French National Convention adopted it as the Republic's anthem in 1795.

Only the first verse (and sometimes the fifth and sixth) and the first chorus are sung today in France. There are some slight historical variations in the lyrics of the song. The following is the version listed at the official website of the French Presidency.

Allons enfants de la Patrie,

Le jour de gloire est arrivé!

Contre nous de la tyrannie,

L'étendard sanglant est levé, (bis)

Entendez-vous dans les campagnes

Mugir ces féroces soldats?

Ils viennent jusque dans vos bras

Égorger vos fils, vos compagnes!

Aux armes, citoyens,

Formez vos bataillons,

Marchons, marchons!

Qu'un sang impur

Abreuve nos sillons!

Que veut cette horde d'esclaves,

De traîtres, de rois conjurés?

Pour qui ces ignobles entraves,

Ces fers dès longtemps préparés? (bis)

Français, pour nous, ah! quel outrage

Quels transports il doit exciter!

C'est nous qu'on ose méditer

De rendre à l'antique esclavage!

Aux armes, citoyens...

Quoi! des cohortes étrangères

Feraient la loi dans nos foyers!

Quoi! Ces phalanges mercenaires

Terrasseraient nos fiers guerriers! (bis)

Grand Dieu! Par des mains enchaînées

Nos fronts sous le joug se ploieraient

De vils despotes deviendraient

Les maîtres de nos destinées!

Aux armes, citoyens...

Tremblez, tyrans et vous perfides

L'opprobre de tous les partis,

Tremblez! vos projets parricides

Vont enfin recevoir leurs prix! (bis)

Tout est soldat pour vous combattre,

S'ils tombent, nos jeunes héros,

La terre en produit de nouveaux,

Contre vous tout prêts à se battre!

Aux armes, citoyens...

Français, en guerriers magnanimes,

Portez ou retenez vos coups!

Épargnez ces tristes victimes,

À regret s'armant contre nous. (bis)

Mais ces despotes sanguinaires,

Mais ces complices de Bouillé,

Tous ces tigres qui, sans pitié,

Déchirent le sein de leur mère!

Aux armes, citoyens...

Amour sacré de la Patrie,

Conduis, soutiens nos bras vengeurs

Liberté, Liberté chérie,

Combats avec tes défenseurs! (bis)

Sous nos drapeaux que la victoire

Accoure à tes mâles accents,

Que tes ennemis expirants

Voient ton triomphe et notre gloire!

Aux armes, citoyens...

(Couplet des enfants)[13]

Nous entrerons dans la carrière

Quand nos aînés n'y seront plus,

Nous y trouverons leur poussière

Et la trace de leurs vertus (bis)

Bien moins jaloux de leur survivre

Que de partager leur cercueil,

Nous aurons le sublime orgueil

De les venger ou de les suivre

Aux armes, citoyens...

Arise, children of the Fatherland,

The day of glory has arrived!

Against us tyranny's

Bloody banner is raised, (repeat)

Do you hear, in the countryside,

The roar of those ferocious soldiers?

They're coming right into your arms

To cut the throats of your sons, your women!

To arms, citizens,

Form your battalions,

Let's march, let's march!

Let an impure blood

Soak our fields!

What does this horde of slaves,

Of traitors and conspiratorial kings want?

For whom are these vile chains,

These long-prepared irons? (repeat)

Frenchmen, for us, ah! What outrage

What fury it must arouse!

It is us they dare plan

To return to the old slavery!

To arms, citizens...

What! Foreign cohorts

Would make the law in our homes!

What! These mercenary phalanxes

Would strike down our proud warriors! (repeat)

Great God! By chained hands

Our brows would yield under the yoke

Vile despots would have themselves

The masters of our destinies!

To arms, citizens...

Tremble, tyrants and you traitors

The shame of all parties,

Tremble! Your parricidal schemes

Will finally receive their reward! (repeat)

Everyone is a soldier to combat you

If they fall, our young heroes,

The earth will produce new ones,

Ready to fight against you!

To arms, citizens...

Frenchmen, as magnanimous warriors,

Bear or hold back your blows!

Spare those sorry victims,

Who arm against us with regret. (repeat)

But not these bloodthirsty despots,

These accomplices of Bouillé,

All these tigers who, mercilessly,

Rip their mother's breast!

To arms, citizens...

Sacred love of the Fatherland,

Lead, support our avenging arms

Liberty, cherished Liberty,

Fight with thy defenders! (repeat)

Under our flags, may victory

Hurry to thy manly accents,

May thy expiring enemies,

See thy triumph and our glory!

To arms, citizens...

(Children's Verse)

We shall enter the (military) career

When our elders are no longer there,

There we shall find their dust

And the trace of their virtues (repeat)

Much less keen to survive them

Than to share their coffins,

We shall have the sublime pride

Of avenging or following them

ADDITIONAL CONTACTS

AGENCE NATIONALE POUR L AMELIORATION DE L HABITAT-provides loans to improve property
www.anah.fr

ARCHITECTS
www.architects.org

BANKS

www.labanquepostale.fr	post office bank
www.credit-foncier.fr	Credit Foncier
www.bnpparibas.fr	BNP Paribas
www.credit-agricole.fr	Credit Agricole
www.banques.fr	The French Banking Federation

CAR HIRE
www.hertz.com
www.avis.com

DIY
www.brico-depot.com
www.bricomarche.com
www.castorama.fr

www.leroymerlin.fr
www.mr-bricolage.fr

EDUCATION
www.education.gouv.fr   MINISTRY OF EDUCATION

ELECTRICITY
www.edf.fr

EMPLOYMENT
www.anpe.fr

www.eures-jobs.com

ENERGY
www.ademe.fr
www.enr.fr

FRANCO BRITISH CHAMBER OF COMMERCE
www.francobritishchamber.com

FRENCH ADMINISTRATION SITE
www.service-public.fr

FRENCH INFORMATION IN ENGLISH
www.connexionfrance.com
www.thelocal.fr
www.angloinfo.com
www.expatica.com

GAS –bottled and tank
www.antargaz.fr
www.totalgaz.fr

GITES
www.gites-de-france.fr

IMMIGRATION AND INTEGRATION
www.ofii.fr
www.omi.social.fr

MONEY TRANSFER COMPANIES
www.fcexchange.com
www.cambridgefx.com
www.foremostcurrencygroup.co.uk

NOTAIRE
www.notaires.fr

REMOVAL COMPANIES
www.burkebros.co.uk

www.anglofrenchremovals.co.uk

TRANSPORT
www.equipement.gouv.fr

TRAVEL
www.eurostar.com
www.eurotunnel.com
www.brittanyferries.com
www.hoverspeed.co.uk
www.poferries.com
www.ryanair.com
www.easyjet.co.uk
www.flybmi.com
www.airfrance.fr
www.ba.com

UNIVERSITY ADMISSION
www.ucas.com

OTHER BOOKS BY EILIDH MCGINNESS

FICTION

HISTORICAL THRILLER

THE CYPHER BUREAU   available   March   2018

WOMAN'S ROMANCE

ONE LAST FLING

CHOOSING LOVE

CAPTURED BY THE WARRIOR QUEEN

WEBSITE www.eilidhmcginness.com

ACKNOWLEDGMENTS

I hope you have found this guide useful. It is great to hear from other Francophiles so please feel free to contact me by email at immo24-7@orange.fr

I work as an independent estate agent in France so if you are interested in properties in the South West of France or if you want to keep up to date with my blog about life in France or French lifestyle news generally please check out my website at http://www.propertysouthwestfrance.co.uk/ or follow me on facebook at Immo24-7.com

Moving to France, a beginner's guide

Printed in Great Britain
by Amazon